Randolph W.B.

THE VENICE STORIES

**The New
Atlantian Library**

The New Atlantian Library
is an imprint of
ABSOLUTELY AMAZING eBOOKS

Published by Whiz Bang LLC, 926 Truman Avenue, Key West, Florida 33040, USA.

Copyright © 2001 by Randolph W.B. Becker
Electronic compilation/paperback edition copyright © 2012 by Whiz Bang LLC.

All rights reserved. No part of this book may be reproduced, scanned, or transmitted in any form or by any means, electronic or mechanical, including photocopying, recording, or any information storage and retrieval system, without permission in writing from the publisher. Please do not participate in or encourage piracy of copyrighted materials in violation of the author's rights. Purchase only authorized ebook editions.

This is a work of fiction. Names, characters, places, and incidents either are the product of the author's imagination or are used fictitiously, and any resemblance to actual persons, living or dead, businesses, companies, events, or locales is entirely coincidental. While the author has made every effort to provide accurate information at the time of publication, neither the publisher nor the author assumes any responsibility for errors, or for changes that occur after publication. Further, the publisher does not have any control over and does not assume any responsibility for author or third-party websites or their contents.

For information contact
Publisher@AbsolutelyAmazingEbooks.com

ISBN-13:978-1492329398
ISBN-10:492329398

The Venice Stories

CONTENTS:

FORWARD	1
The UMBRELLA	3
THE TREE	15
THE SUNSET	31
THE SEASONS	35
THE ROOM	51
THE LOVERS	61
THE JOURNEY	73
THE HAND	91
THE GIFT	101
THE FIGHT	117
THE CITY	135
THE CHURCH	153

FORWARD

These stories combine three of my favorite things . . . people, storytelling, and Venezia. However, if you asked me in what priority I would rank the three, I would place surprises as number one – the surprises I find in people, stories, and Venice.

These stories would have been functionally impossible without some very important people: my wife, Elissa, who offered me the time to write; my daughters Suki, Lee, Lizzie, and Ericka, who are constant sources of inspiration; the congregation of the Williamsburg Unitarian Universalists who allowed me my sabbatical; and the folks at the Eli Lilly Foundation who made this time of Clergy Renewal financially possible. I offer my humblest thanks to all of them.

These stories would have been essentially impossible without the people and stories of Venice: Mrs. Cervellii, my Venetian landlady; the two barbers at their shop at Guglie; the grocer who sold me all my Pejo bottled water, my wine-merchant who refilled the emptied Pejo bottles with good wine; Rosella, the Venetian shop-keeper I met on my plane ride; all of my friends at Iguana and Fontana and Antico Mola and Pizzeria Tre Archi who kept me fed on those days when I did not want to cook or when I wanted to observe people, tell stories, or live like a Venetian; and even the civil servants, the boat men and women, the postal clerks, and the police (Civile and Questura) who always treated me, the foreigner,

1

professionally, kindly, and warmly. I offer my warmest thanks to all of them.

But most of all, these stories would have been thematically impossible without Venezia, Queen of the Adriatic. I offer profound thanks that such a place exists.

THE UMBRELLA

He first saw the umbrella as it was being placed into the luggage bin of his flight to Venice. It was that distinctive.

True, it was rolled up, and all he could see was its color.

He could not tell who put it into the bin - was it a man, a woman, someone helping someone else?

But, there it was, a yellow which seared the eyeball with a laser-like precision. He had never seen anything that radiantly yellow.

≈≈≈

But, then it was gone, in the flurry of closed overhead bins.

Travel is, even in its most luxurious modes, a dislocation. On the average trans-Atlantic flight endured in economy, dislocation often refers not only to own's spiritual experience but also to one's spinal experience. He felt out of time, out of place, out of himself. By the time the plane landed, his focus was thoroughly on his creaking frame. When the bins were opened he missed a chance to see whose hand reached for the umbrella.

But he found himself musing about why the umbrella had captured his imagination. He had even dreamed about it during his restless sleep on the plane, with a Busby Berkeley style musical piece of beauties surrounding an umbrella of the same hue, the centerpiece of an amazingly symmetrical circle of human flesh.

The Venice Stories

≈≈≈

Ah, Venice ... Venezia ... city of continuities, city of history, city of mysteries. As he aged, he found the more recent trips had become not just times of new experiences but also times of review of past experiences. He was becoming a walking equivalent of the omnipresent guidebooks. "Here, on my right, I will see the place where I first glimpsed San Marco," "In the next block is the remnant of my favorite osteria," "On the Ponte delle Guglie, I once saw Sophia Loren."

When these thoughts came to his mind this time, he wondered to himself if his days of new experiences were coming to an end. Was it all memories from here on? Is that what all those old people did, who sat somewhere, and sat, and sat — stop having current experiences?

The busyness of arrival, immigration, transfers, check-in, and acclimation all took their time and their toll. His senses were dull, his mind distant, his memories clouded. He knew the antidote to all of the jet-lag and foreign-presence was a walk, even in the light rain, and so he headed toward San Marco. Suddenly he saw, moving around the corner ahead of him, the umbrella! It blazed into his reality like a lightning bolt, energizing his step as he tried to catch up to his query. Yet, as he knew, the passage narrows at this point, slowing the crowd, and then disperses into a number of optional routes to San Marco. His pace could not become quick enough. Found, and then lost – the opposite of the usual fate of an umbrella.

But that sighting of the umbrella, even as it faded into the distance, had created a wave of excitement in him. The encyclopedia of memories was suddenly shelved and all of his senses became present. He felt alive, really alive. He felt young. He felt vital.

≈≈≈

As energized as he felt, he found that his energy did not last long. By the time of an early dinner, he felt more exhausted than he had ever felt on a first night in this city. He even passed up his usual option of staying in San Marco as the predicted full moon should have been rising above the Basilica.

Again, his sleep was filled with images of the umbrella. This time he witnessed a long progression of London-looking businessmen, each with black overcoat, black bowler, black attaché, and one of the electric yellow umbrellas, neatly rolled, in one hand. Periodically, but in unison, each man on the street would stop, and swap the attaché and the umbrella from hand to hand.

In the morning he felt more rested, but not really rested.

His stamina seemed to be failing, and he wondered if maybe some flu was the culprit. Yet, he did not ache, he was not feverish. His appetite seemed constant, which pleased him in this city of seafood delights. Maybe, with age, he thought, travel is that much harder.

≈≈≈

Later, while cutting through Dorsoduro toward the Rialto to avoid the crowds of Sestier San Marco, he saw the umbrella again. This time it was open, even though it was only a cloudy day, with no rain at all.

Aha, he realized, a tour guide's umbrella, the beacon

The Venice Stories

for travelers in the guide's charge. And what a great beacon it was. Now he could see it in all of its brilliance. Yellow, with a small, repeating pattern of blue cats, but these were not house cats. These were regal lions, the lions of Saint Mark. Fierce, strong, sacred.

His eye then traveled down the shaft of the umbrella to the hand holding it. It was a feminine hand which beckoned his eye further to behold the whole person.

What he saw was a woman not that much younger than he, but what a woman. She was as electric as her yellow umbrella. And she looked like those lions — fierce, strong — and in her beauty, sacred. If the umbrella had penetrated his fascination, she penetrated his soul.

But, before he knew what was happening, she was leading the group away and a mass of others had swarmed between him and her. His feet seemed to be glued to the spot even if the way had been clear. Nothing this new, nothing this powerful, nothing this memorable had happened to him in ... well, he could not remember when.

That night he dreamt again of the umbrella, but this time it had become a giant beach umbrella, shading him and her on an idyllic tropical beach all their own. Magically, while their faces looked as now, their naked bodies were those of young people. They glistened and gleamed in the sweaty heat of the circle of shade. They talked and touched. And into the interior of the dream he sank further and further, leaving him at last more soundly asleep than he had known for days.

In the morning, he could think of little other than finding the umbrella and more so the umbrella's holder.

His mind began to calculate where he thought he might see her. Was she conducting a tour for a single group, so she was unlikely to be seen again in the same place? Or was she conducting tours for new groups each day, so she was likely to be seen again in the same place?

Should he begin his own tours of the city's most famous sights, hoping his path would cross hers? Should he choose one place of prominence, assuming that she would eventually pass him?

After over an hour of such musings, he realized that she was unlikely to stop by his hotel's breakfast room. So, he hastily retreated to his room to prepare for his day, HIS day, HER day.

≈≈≈

He finally chose an end row table outside at Café Florian, reasoning that she and her charges would eventually pass through the grand plaza at the heart of the city. So, for hours, he sat facing into the passing crowd. He enjoyed the passing parade of people, of young women whose charm once would have caught his fancy, young men trying to catch the eye of those young women, young men trying to catch the eye of other young men, older people worrying their purses and wallets through the square, tourists wearing more cameras than clothes, haltering steps with canes of Venetians of a certain age. Each person a delight, but not the delight he sought.

A salad and two coffees later, just as midday was becoming afternoon, as Venezianos reappeared to un-shutter closed shops, he thought he caught a glimpse of yellow at the far end, coming from the direction of the

Rialto. Was it the umbrella? He stood suddenly, almost spilling his coffee. Was it?

The thickening crowd blocked his view for a moment, but then, like the Red Sea before Moses, it opened the whole length of the square and there it was, the umbrella, and there she was, the woman.

Should he move, try to get closer? Should he wait to see where they were headed? "Il conto, per favore," he called to the waiter, trying to prepare to leave. He hastily over-tipped, but did not even notice. When he turned back from the transaction, he looked back to where the umbrella had been, and it was gone.

He was desolate. What had he done? He could have just thrown the money down and left. He could have paid attention to his query, sitting patiently to see what was unfolding. He could have ... he could have seen her up close, maybe make eye contact, maybe ...

He scanned the far corners of the Piazza. Under the arcades. Toward the Campanile. Nothing yellow! Nothing!

He sat down, tired, sad, empty.

≈ ≈ ≈

Then he realized that he was in shade, and looking up to see what cloud had robbed him of the sun, all he could see was yellow, a yellow more brilliant than the sun itself.

She was standing right there, in front of him, having come from behind him, to lecture her assembled tour. She was speaking in English with that almost erotic overtone of native Italian.

He did not hear the words she was saying, only the rhythm of her voice, washing over him like a fountain of youth. O, she was so wonderful, everything he could ever create in a woman of his fantasies.

Now the tourists were asking her questions, most trivial seeming in nature to him. He wanted to ask her some real questions, questions such as "What is the most important moment of your life?", "What does it mean to you to be an Italian?", "What do you dream about in those moments just before arising?", "What are you doing for dinner tonight?"

Apparently someone had asked either a particularly hard or a particularly stupid question for suddenly her voice came to a halt. She paused, as if to consider her words perfectly. Then, she began again, "Well, in that case, the Doge would hava probably offered an alternateeva to the Council without any of the foreign sense to it. Appearances would be more important than, the, ah, realities. Yes?" And then (did he only imagine it?) she turned, looked him straight in the eye, and winked a conspiratorial wink, followed by a smile almost Da Vinci in content.

By the time the look and the smile had registered, she had moved on. He rose, and trailed the group for a while, listening from afar to her voice drifting from within her circle. When they entered the Palazzo Ducale, he held back, watching her almost ceremonially close the umbrella and wrap it shut. As she and the umbrella entered inside, it was as if a sudden eclipse had descended on the city.

Now, he wondered, should he wait outside, like some school-boy crushed with love, or should he retreat to savor the joys of this day, knowing that probably tomorrow he could again encounter her in the Piazza.

That night he dreamed another dream. He and she were sitting in the Piazza, but between Florian and Quadri there was only their table. Above them stood the yellow umbrella, now a large shade for their table. The dream began in the morning, she and he talking over coffee. When the dream noon came, they were sitting closer, intently looking into each other's eyes. By afternoon, with the sun peaking under the umbrella, their fingers were touching. As the evening shadows lengthened, a full moon arose over the Basilica bathing them in a lunar white light, but neither of them seemed to notice as hands intertwined, one pair on each side of the now empty dinner plates. At long last, the two stood, and she, with grace, took the umbrella and transformed it into its usual size, folding it as he had observed her do earlier. Then, with one arm around each other, they strolled off in the direction of his hotel. Just as they reached the cover of the arcade and he lowered his face to kiss her beautiful lips, suddenly the whole space was filled with the screech of sirens ... wait, not the dream space, his whole hotel room.

The signals of acqua alta, the dangerous combination of wind, moon, and tide which would bring flooded walkways to the city in the morning. The wind whipped by his window in a way different from the previous nights. Gradually the sound of increasing rain was added to the wind.

The Piazza would not be a place to sit. At best, a narrow passage of raised platforms would allow only the most important foot traffic to move. The whole city would be disrupted. Boats rerouted or canceled. Tourists asked to stay away.

Would he ever see her again?

He fell asleep in the fatigue of sadness.

The morning dawned as fiercely as predicted. The wind was still up. The rain continued. The hotel clerk suggested that the only real destination for the day was the train station to leave, but "Signore, it will not be an easy journey to the station."

How could he leave? His air ticket still read more than a week away. He had things to do in Venice. He had to see her again, catch another wink perhaps, maybe venture a conversation.

Yet, part of him felt like it had already left. He felt drained, almost lifeless.

His feelings of unwellness were not helped by his insistence at the first low tide to battle his way through the wind and the rain to the Piazza, just to assure himself that there was no point in being there in wait. He could not remember wind this strong in his beloved city before. Returning to the hotel, he was chilled. Even the warm soup of dinner did not remove the chill. It did not feel as much like a chill of the body, but more the chill of an omen, like an icy stare of the universe into his spirit.

His sleep was punctuated with segments of a recurring dream. Again and again, he saw his beloved walking along the raised platforms in San Marco, her umbrella above her head. Suddenly a gust of wind would come from behind her, fill the umbrella, and lift her away, lift her into the clouds and away, until at last a battered umbrella would tumble into the flood of the Piazza. Over and over again. In the morning he found himself tangled in his bedclothes, alternating between intense sweats and intense chills. He chose to have the expensive full, hot breakfast delivered to his room. It worked as a restorative.

Opening his shutters, he looked out upon a city that looked like nature had been a scrub-maid, leaving a brilliantly clean view beneath a sunny sky with only a slight gust of wind to remind one of the storm. Through his aches and chills he dressed, and by mid-morning was ready to take some sun in hope of a full recovery of his energy and well-being.

The Piazza was nearly empty except for crews removing walkways, cleaning the stones, making it ready for normal life again. He strolled past the Doge's Palace, on toward San Zaccaria, slowly lifting himself over Ponte d' Paglia, and audibly sighing his own resignation on looking at the bridge to his left. Suddenly he caught a glimpse of bright, electric yellow ahead. His eyes opened wide. His pace quickened. Until he came to a complete stop. There was the umbrella, alone, abandoned, with one of its ribs bent, propped against the railing of the Motoscafo stop. Its life was over.

≈≈≈

Three days later, the rain suddenly returned. Angelina, a young woman of sorrow, made her way from her apartment to take the boat to the Cimitero on San Michele, for her weekly visit to her mother. The months since her death had brought Angelina little relief from the pain of loss. Each visit was one more reminder of that pain, and one more reminder of her feeling of the loss of love.

The rain began again and she cursed her inattention in not bringing an umbrella. Looking for something to shield herself once she disembarked on San Michele, she spotted an abandoned umbrella leaning on the railing. Its broken rib meant that it opened lopsided, but it still provided a good oval of protection from the rain. She was concerned that such a bright yellow umbrella might seem inappropriate in the cemetery, but her mother had always loved yellow; even today she was carrying a bouquet of bright Narcisi to decorate the grave of her desolation.

At San Michele, she slowly walked beneath the sheltering yellow canopy down the path toward her mother's resting place. Dropping to her knees, using the wrapping of the bouquet to protect her slacks, she placed the flowers at the grave, and then watered them with her tears. Minutes became an hour until her mourning was interrupted by the nearby sounds of workers closing a small grave. She overheard their chatter. "So sad. No one came at all. No one. Some American. Heart failure, I heard. All alone, down by San Marco."

When they were done and had left, she slowly rose, and from the bouquet she took one brilliantly yellow flower. In leaving the cemetery she stopped at the fresh grave. Shestared at the space with no name to which no one had come. Then she placed the single, bright, alomost electric flower on the grave, for she knew what it was to be alone, cut off from love. Looking back at it, it looked like a small umbrella of brightness <u>against</u> a world full or rain.

THE TREE

When he was seven, he thought he had invented *déjà vu*. It happened in that little garden aside the Vaporetto stop for San Marco, the vest-pocket piece of nature and solitude so close to the center of a city renowned for triumph over nature and little solitude.

As he and his family strolled the little garden, a single tree took hold of his imagination, and he felt as if he had known the tree before. It was a feeling so overpowering that he had to speak of it. Of course, what a seven year old might say of such insistent memories of a past reality was limited by his use of language, and "Mommy, I used to be here with that tree." was the best he could express.

"Of course, dear," his mother replied, with a tone uncertain of either dismissal or affirmation.

"No, Mommy, I mean I have been with that tree before, just like I am now!"

"Yes, of course, dear," she repeated, "like when you were three."

"When I was three?"

It was then that he learned his *déjà vu* had been but the quirk of his parents' summer plans. His father, a professor at a small university in New England, and his mother, minister to an even smaller Universalist church in the university town, shared the common gift of extended summer vacations. In a four-year sequence, they would rotate between Venice, London, Paris, and inexplicably Thun, Switzerland. (It would be years later that he would

The Venice Stories

learn that Thun was in the rotation because it was the one city in which neither of his parents could do research, so it was seen as an almost sinfully indulgent total vacation, allowed only one year in four.)

When he was but an infant, not yet even given a digit to measure his age, he had been wheeled about with so many others in their prams in London. At one, he had played with *les enfants* in Paris. At two, the toddler has negotiated a summer of careful steps on cobblestones and near misses into the lake at Thun. His third year, and his fourth summer had brought them back to Venice, the first summer somewhat planted in his memory.

"Don't you remember, dear," his mother asked, "about that tree?"

"No, should I?"

"O, it was when you were three, and for some unknown reason your father had taken it into his mind that the summer would be the time to toilet-train you. So, here in Venice, we tried to teach you to use the potty. And you were such a quick learner. Or was it that we were quick learners?" she paused, and looked skyward briefly. "One day, as we waited for the next boat to the Lido, so you could go play in the sand, which you loved to do, you suddenly got that look on your face that told father and me that you need your potty. But, what to do? All I could think of was to get you into the park, beside a nice tree, and let you relieve yourself there. And that's what you did, and that's your tree."

"My tree?"

"Well, if your were a dog, we would say that you had

marked it as your own, so to speak."

"My tree."

"You and that tree have a relationship in your memory – a part of the web of your being."

"My tree!"

And so the pact was sealed, in action and memory, in story and affirmation. He and the tree. The tree. His tree!

In four years, when he was eleven and a bit more scampish than some, he returned with his family once more to Venice. Late one night, on the guise of wanting some independence from his family (who now numbered five, with the addition of his twin-sisters (also products, it would seem, of the city of islands), he took the long, slow ride down the canal to San Marco, and then, in the quiet stillness of a fog-shrouded night, he went to his tree, and once again marked his domain, set his limit, declare himself to be.

≈≈≈

A fifteen-year-old on a family trip, with parents who have increasingly become objects of embarrassment and sisters who, at seven years old, were even more embarrassing, finds little reason to consider such a summer a gift of any kind. He was no exception. No, he did not want to play in the sand of the Lido with his sisters. No, he did not think the sunsets were the most beautiful things in the world if it meant sitting in one place for an hour watching a darkening sky. No, he did not want to see how glass was made (one more time). No, he did not want to explore the canals, especially with the high-pitched squeals of his sisters at every new vista calling attention to this foreign family. And most especially no, he did not even want to think about the idea that Venice had often served as his parents' inspiration for family increase. This was a summer to be endured, at best.

Endured, that was, until one day when he had left that embarrassing lot at the vaporetto dock for a moment and wandered back into the garden. He had almost forgotten about the garden in his adolescent pre-occupation with the present. But there it was again, his tree, and he felt his cheeks burn with embarrassment at the memory of not only how he and that tree had formed their relationship, but also in how he had so unspeakably renewed that relationship the last time he was here.

But his memories were interrupted by the sight of the young woman standing beneath the shade of the tree, his tree. Studying a guidebook with a perplexed look on her face, she could have passed (in his sight) for any of the too-many Madonnas he had been forced to view over all the years. Hers was tenderness, eagerness, beauty, quiet ... in a word, innocence. And that innocence grabbed his heart and made him less than innocent in an instant. In that moment he had gone from observer of life to lover of life.

Summoning a courage he did not know he had and which since he has often wished he had again, he walked to her side, and with authority said, "Scuzi, Ho bisogno dell'assistenza" not knowing he had just asked her for help rather than the more gallant offer of help he supposed he was making.

She turned from her guidebook, and while her mouth made the sounds of "Are you English?", her eyes sounded all the strings of all the music of all the centuries ever heard. All he could respond was a definitive "Huh?"

"I asked if you were English," she offered, "but now I suspect you are American."

"Yes, American," he was able to say, as the start of a conversation o-so-deliciously long and o-so-painfully cut short by his father's summons to the arriving boat. But in the brief sentences he learned she was a Scot, on holiday, staying near the Academia, to be there two more weeks, while she learned he was American, on holiday, staying near the Rialto, to be there three more weeks, and both learning that tomorrow at noon each would be at the tree.

Not wishing to be late, he arrived in the garden shortly after 11:30, and she, equally afraid of missing the appointed hour, already awaited him. Theirs was a midday full of words and silences, of glances and glances away, and finally of a hand-in-hand stroll across the Academia Bridge to his watery and her walkway return to family. That noon became the first of many noons caught in the excitement of connection.

All too soon, it was time for her to return with her family to that region above Hadrian's Wall; their final 12 o'clock together was not a noon, but a midnight, when, under the tree, he and she shared each's first real kiss of passion and romance. Over too soon, but long enough to last a lifetime.

The next day he stood by the tree again, now fuller and emptier than he had ever felt before. Life as a child was behind; life as an adult was ahead. He could feel it in every fiber of his being.

The Venice Stories

But, in the fiber of the world, strong forces were conspiring to make him more of a man and she more of a woman than either would have dreamt of under that tree. In four years, the presence of either of them in Italy would have been impossible. The cycle was broken. Venice, London, Paris, Thun, became a sequence of the past.

Against a backdrop of hostilities, their letters crossed the vast ocean; with each passing note their bond grew deeper, stronger, more urgent.

By the time his next vacation in Venice was due, he wore khaki rather than vacation clothes, and his middays were filled with order rather than ardor. While still young in years, he was becoming older by the day, as he joined countless others in the slow pursuit of peace across Europe. The continent that had so often given him rest and relaxation now asked for its recompense in his commitment and toil. Here, there, at various places between the engagements with the enemy that required total concentration and elicited total fear, he would spy some tree, or remnant of tree, at the edge of the battlefield, and he would remember better times, and that certain tree.

She, in the call of duty as well, served as a nurse, now posted outside of London, in care of those returned from the front by reason of the worst kind of injuries. As a surgical and recovery room nurse, she saw all the horrors of war permanently scarred onto the lives of young men. So many lives touched, maimed, destroyed. And still, through the worst of it, his letters came. Sometimes several in a single post, and other times weeks apart. With each one came a small drawing beside his name, a simple outline of a tree, that spoke more of him to her than his name. She had her own forest, captured on the pages of the saved letters that filled her box, a forest of hope, of promise, of love.

He returned to Italy by way of Sicily, with Patton. He flowed north with the advancing tide of liberation, crying with joy and with loss at each new town; would anything of the past be able to survive through such destruction? At long last, he was but a few hours from his beloved Venice, a few hours in peace that is, when he caught a small piece of shrapnel in his left leg.

She received the letter from the hospital ship before she received the letter from the field hospital. Such was the news of those days, when time was often out of joint. Her first news of the wound was of its healing, not its injury. Yet, even the news of health sat her down to weep silently, all the more so for there, there on the bottom of the page, a little more shaky than usual, was the tree.

He finally spoke the words his heart had known twelve years earlier when they exchanged the vows of marriage that late autumn day. They had both had but one requirement of the simple ceremony in rural Scotland: that from where they stood, they could see a tree. And so it was that as each said, "I do", the nearly bare branches of a stand of trees blessed their union far more than could any clergy.

She was more to him than simply an adolescent love affair. Her work as a nurse suited her, for she was one of those caring people who seemed to have unlimited energy

The Venice Stories

to give to others. In her care, pain was eased, and a future possible. She continued to receive letters from many of the patients in her care at the military hospital, usually containing phrases about how she had made life not only bearable but desirable. To him, however, she was more than simply the caring nurse. For him, she was an earthy rootedness, a connection to all things permanent, sustained, supported. How often he would feel some tremor of anxiety well up in him only to have it subside at the mere touch or sight of her.

And he, to her, was like the mast of a great ship, hewn from some tall tree, full of the energy that propelled them through life. In the midst of the great gales of misfortune, he stood true, strong, certain. Such was his character, shared with others as well, of one who had withstood much and was the stronger for it. He might bend, but he would not break, and in her pre-sleep consideration of each day, his wife always felt assured of the morning knowing she slept beside such a source of enduring strength.

Yet, he knew his strength would be nothing if he did not have her anchoring roots to sustain him; she knew here nurturing spirit would seem to be for nothing if she could not sustain a spirit as tall and true as his. They were two forces of the same organism.

He, as a schoolteacher, and she, as a part-time nurse, had the vacations for travel, but hardly the money, especially with the arrival of their son and then their daughter.

One might think he had adopted the manner of the

times in nicknaming his son "Bud", but it was not a contraction for Buddy. The boy, from his earliest days, seemed like something constantly coming into being, like an eternal bud on the family tree. Bud was the one who always brought home the newest of whatever was appearing: tadpoles, peonies, fireflies, transistor radio, instamatic camera ... life was always unfolding for Bud. For a father, it felt like a constant race, to keep up with the boy, a race well worth running. If his wife kept him grounded, his son gave him wings, wings into the future. In his son he saw so much of himself that naturally went undeveloped until summoned by this sprig of youth.

His daughter, Grace, was no less a wonder to him. He was glad he had a daughter and a son, and so did not need to think about which boy or which girl he liked better out of a lot. Each child in his or her own way was so special that he was not backed into a forced fatherly choice of preference. If Bud was something constantly coming into being, then Grace was a rhythmic pulsing of coming and going, always holding promise of a season yet to be while remembering a season already past. She wanted to know what something had been, and she wanted to know why it was not that something anymore, and she wanted to know what it would become now. For every measure of grounding he got from his wife, and every sense of flight he receive from his son, he gained an equal measure of perspective and pacing from Grace. In due time he came to understand the concept of things happening in due time.

It was not until their tenth anniversary that they could return to their beloved Venice. With a vivacious nine and an introspective eight-year-old in tow, they mounted the familiar bridges, road the remembered boats, but had little time alone to return midday or midnight to their garden, and their tree. They saw it survived well, growing in their absence even without their blessed and blessing presence.

Years rolled into decades, replacing the four-year cycle with the longer rhythm of modern life. If anything, his relationship with his wife deepened as they weathered the storm of adolescent children and the '60s. Often he could stand fast and strong only with her steadying presence at his side; often she felt she would have been torn from her roots if he had not be his stalwart self. They learned more about living as one, enriching each other.

Bud grew, sprouting upward with almost weed-like speed, his body energetic with basketball and track, his mind energized with Salinger and Kerouac and Gibran. A beard came and went, hair lengthened, music loudened, but Bud was still Bud, a promise beyond measure to his father, a hope into the future.

Grace also grew, her arms and legs lengthened, and spread forth like branches of a wide canopy. She studied ballet and then modern dance. She began to act, and took to the stage like it had been her birthright. The senior play was her acting triumph, as she had the lead in *Lysistrata*. The role blended perfectly with her growing interest in law and social action. So often, late at night, father and daughter, after all the others had gone to their sleep, would argue points of law and ethics, in a search for not only agreement but also continuity of human meaning.

Ahead for them all was the time of great harvest, of

dreams coming to fruition, or so it seemed. Each in the little circle of family giving so much to each other, and each also giving so much to the outer world. Energy built on energy, caring built on caring.

Their twentieth anniversary was scheduled for Venice, but the shrapnel their son met in the Mekong Delta found a deeper mark than the leg wound of his father. On their anniversary, they gathered instead beneath a large tree in their hometown while bugle and rifle echoed death's reality across the wide valley. The days, the months, the years after that were, for many a season, a blur, a silence, a numbing. He taught, but wondered about the point of all education. She cared for surgical patients, but wondered about the value of all acts of caring. They sat, holding hands, beneath the leafy canopy of their backyard, and wondered about whether a far-distant tree had been only a fantasy, an illusion like the illusion of permanence, of continuity, of meaning. Were all the buds on all the trees just cruel jokes of promise? A decade seemed to disappear into longing; they were there for each other, but barely took notice of that reality. She felt uprooted, disconnected. He felt splintered, rootless. The promised spring had turned into winter before all the joys of summer and fall had been realized.

On their thirtieth anniversary, with the insistence of their daughter, they returned to the city of their dreams which now almost frightened them with the possibility of being only an empty promise. But on that first day, still tired with jet-lag, they made their way at noon to the small garden, and standing beneath the tree, their tree, two

The Venice Stories

fifteen-year-olds full of hope and wonder and love emerged into the bright sun once again. Again they could stroll the Piazza, with eyes only for each other, and eyes clouded only with the tears of joy. It felt so foreign to them to feel this good, this full, this worthy of joy, but rather than shrink from it in fear, they embraced the feelings like long-lost friends. To be alive, to be alive in Venice, to be alive in Venice with each other!

It was only a small lesion, the doctor said. Easily biopsied, and equally easily removed at the same time. But they both held their breath for the pathologist's report, and with the report lost all breath whatsoever. Malignant. Aggressive. Exploratory. Metastasized. Chemo. Radiation. The words flowed on over months, until the doctors had run out of words, and turned her care over to her fellow nurses. In the early stages of treatment, she had still been planning the next trip, which would have been the third of their renewed four-year cycles. By the end of the chemotherapy, she knew she was not going to Venice again, but did not tell him for she sensed that he needed that hope. He had not spoken to her of how he doubted she would see Venice again for he sensed that she needed that hope. Now each of them longed for a simple symbol to remind them of what they would always have, but strangely in all the years they had never photographed the garden nor the tree.

She died on a barren Tuesday in mid-winter, and on a Saturday in early spring most of her ashes were buried, in a plot near their son, in front of a large granite marker that bore her name and dates, and only his name. The carving of a single tree above their names in the eternal stone seemed etched into the fabric of the universe itself. No other words were engraved in the stone, for what words could convey more than that simple image.

≈ ≈ ≈

That summer, he once again walked from the vaporetto dock to the small garden, and at midday on the middle day of the year, he quietly spread some of her ashes at the base of the tree, and stood in silent memory until later bells of the day summoned him onward. He felt like he had discharged a duty, an obligation, but in doing so had assumed an even greater, unspoken one. However, rather being worn like a burden, it felt like an honor, an honor he did not yet recognize.

He also felt like he finally had something he had been missing in himself all these years. As he had placed the ashes around the roots of their tree, he suddenly felt the roots, for the first time, as his own, a part of his own being, and not something brought to him. Her roots were now his, and what this gave him he did not know and what this would require of him he could not guess.

≈ ≈ ≈

The bond of father and daughter now intertwined in new ways: he, with his new sense of both roots and strength, coupled with Grace's rhythmic being now enhanced with a more daring edge, a piece of her brother now living through her. She pushed herself and him in new thoughts and activities, he grounded her in tradition and familiarity and trust. It was like they were keeping alive in the two of them what had been the work of the

The Venice Stories

four before. They worked with what remained. He was both parents – she was both children.

This was not easy, since she had long since left home, left the hometown, and now taught law some 100 miles away. But, with an openness to computers their lively discussions stretched across many a cybernight which neither could have thought endurable alone.

≈≈≈

He sensed immediately that something was wrong. His daughter's partner, a deeply caring and spiritual woman who wrote poetry he admired, was weeping. The telephone call was too late in the night. He caught the major words ... car, truck, hospital ... and within half an hour was en route to his daughter's bedside, covering the two-hour's drive in almost wordless suspension. Five hours later, when the last tube had been disconnected, the three of them shared silent space together – the father, the daughter, the lover. Once more in the presence of death, the living holding hands with the dead and with each other forming what felt like a too-small circle. Eyes that thought they contained no more tears cried again, and the familiar numbness crept from the edges and filtered into his spirit. The rhythms of his seasons had been disrupted. He was adrift in the sea of loss. He was no longer aware, much less assured, of his own strength. All seemed dark before him, and a chill wind blew through leafless branches.

The catalogs came, from Elderhostel, and the Alumni Association, and the community arts council, all offering "the chance of a lifetime to explore Venice". Like so much of his mail, they ended up in the recycling bin, glanced at at best. To travel to the mailbox now seemed like a long journey, much less as far away as the travel agent; beyond was out of the question.

Then, one day, he realized that he was gazing at the calendar with an intensity he had not known for more months than he dare remember. Who had even put this current calendar here? He could not remember. But on that January morning, he realized that it was now 2000, a changing of the digits, a point of perspective. To himself he thought, "I must see it once again, as the millennia change," and surprised himself with the thought.

≈≈≈

On the middle day of the year, at midday, he stood once more in Venice, in the little garden, in the shade of a tree, the tree, his tree, their tree, and he wept. But this time he wept not for loss, but for appreciation. He wept for having known love beyond words and bounds and death. He wept for all the joy his son and daughter had brought him. He wept for all this and the many suddenly remembered and remarkable events of his life which now filled his being to overflowing. The flow of tears washed down his face, dripped from his chin, and watered the roots of the tree.

The distant ring of bells again recalled him to the present. The afternoon was progressing. As he made his way back toward the dock, he turned and smiled at the tree.

He never made it home. At the airport in the States he suffered a massive heart attack and died instantly. His dates were also carved into the stone, and his ashes were

The Venice Stories

buried beneath the tree of etched stone, in the shadow of other trees. No one remained to take some of his ashes to a foreign land where a small garden sits near a boat dock.

≈≈≈

In late August, a mother with her young son, sought the refuge of the garden in Venice as he urgently pranced in need of relief. Once the urgency was relieved, he turned to his mother and said "Mommy, I used to be here with this tree."

"Of course not, dear, you've never been here before," his mother replied.

"No, Mommy, I mean I have been with this tree before, when I was an old man.

THE SUNSET

He's just one of those guys.

Always, and I mean always, gets it wrong.

Ask him who he's voting for, and the other candidate is a sure thing.

Let him give you directions only if you want to go somewhere else.

He was the one mentioned in *The Times* who got on the AMTRAK train to go to Philly, and found himself on the first non-stop Acela Express to Washington.

When he got married, he showed up at the wrong church.

If it weren't so often tragic, it would be funny.

Sure, there was that time in London, the incident with the car when he almost got it right. He did remember to look right, but got hit by a German tourist coming down the wrong side of the road.

And that time he re-boarded the wrong cruise ship in St. Thomas, and the one he got on was the one that then had a run of dysentery.

The year that the IRS stopped allowing credit card interest as a deduction, he still deducted his credit card interest but forgot his mortgage interest.

His extensive Beta-Max film collection is legendary.

(Don't even whisper *four track*!)

Retraining as a linotype operator in the late 1970s ... buying a Yugo ... buying a 10-year-old Kaypro so he could

The Venice Stories

get started in computers ... selling the Starbucks stock his family gave him ...

And every time, I mean every time, he said the same thing: "I guess I was wrong. I am so, so sad."

Wagered on Pete Rose's getting into the Hall of Fame ... "so, so sad."

Bought a Rolex from a street vendor on 2nd Avenue ... "so, so sad."

Went to his college reunion a year late ... "so, so sad."

Forgot his own kid's name at her Christening ... "so, so sad."

(Wait a minute, I need to wipe my tears ... I always cry when I laugh this hard.)

But, what is most amazing about him is that none of this gets him down, none of it.

You would think that such monumental failure of judgment would result in some level of depression, but his "so, so sad" was seemingly ironic. He always grinned as he said it, always. I wonder what goes on in that head of his. I do.

Well, the latest I heard he was heading for Venice.

I asked him "Why Venice?" and he said he figured it was one place where he would not have any possibility of being hit by a car. I didn't have the heart to tell him my vision involving him and the Grand Canal.

I didn't hear about the trip directly, but only through his wife (marrying her may have been the only right thing he ever did!).

It seems that they had gotten to Venice with only minor problems. That is, minor if you call going to the wrong terminal to change planes at De Gaulle and therefore arriving in Venice 6 hours late minor.

The hotel was OK considering he had asked for a room without a shower thinking that would mean they would get a bathtub.

Actually, most of the time went quite well. From that bumpy start, the two weeks began to proceed according to schedule.

But, somewhere in the beginning of the second week, he began to complain of some intestinal pain. They both figured it was from the food or the water or something simple. Wrong!

By the following day he was writhing on the bed, screaming bloody murder. An ambulance was summoned, and he was taken to hospital. To have intense abdominal pain in a city where the ambulances use a water route over waves and wakes kept his pattern alive.

The diagnosis was quick - acute appendicitis, with fears of it bursting at any moment. "Don't rush anything!" he asked, about a minute before it did burst. Emergency surgery followed immediately, complicated only by his own mistaken assumption about one of the pre-surgery questions to which he answered "none" when a severe allergy should have been mentioned.

His recovery was far from certain. He was in the ICU of the hospital, hooked up to too many things, being pumped full of antibiotics to fight the spread of the peritoneal infection. He lapsed in and out of reality, fueled by surges of fever and then chills.

His wife was by his side the whole time. She said he

The Venice Stories

mumbled a lot. Then would suddenly fall very silent. She is not sure which frightened her more, his ramblings or his silences.

It was about four days into her vigil that she noticed his chart indicated that his fever was abating. His fluids in and out were improving, and all the signs were good.

It was at this point that he opened his eyes, I mean she said he opened them wider than she had ever seen them opened. He stared out the window, and then pointed to the horizon across the water, to the strands of sunlight and colored clouds. Then he began to rant.

"It's the end. It's a sign. I'm ready to go, Lord, I'm ready. I see my sunset. I see my sunset. I see the light. I'm coming. I'm coming."

"But dear," his wife corrected him, "you've got yourself turned around again. That's the sunrise."

"I guess I was wrong. I am so, so . . . glad," was all he could say.

"Funny," she told me, "he was not smiling as he said it."

THE SEASONS

Inverno

She would have to have that kind of parents. The ones who think a trip somewhere is better than staying home anywhere. The ones who forget to look at the larger calendar and only understood time in terms of school holidays. The ones who haven't a clue about the inner life of a sixteen-year-old daughter.

Add to that her new boyfriend left behind, her ability to bring only a shamefully few outfits, the long boringly-proper boat trip across a grey Atlantic, a night train with *strangers*, and now two weeks in a city thoroughly without charm. Christmas in Venice. New Year's in Venice. Winter in Venice. The introduction of 1936 to her life was more like a requiem than a celebration.

No, she did not want to join her father at the gallery. No, she did not want to join her mother at the library. No, No, No.

One of the advantages of the steamer had been that there was plenty of steam. Their inner stateroom had been almost sauna-like (long before she knew what a sauna was), and against the bracing winds of the ocean it was a welcome sanctuary. The steam railway carriage offered a similar respite from the chilling winds of France and Switzerland. But here, in this dark, damp, dank city, warmth seemed to me meted out in drops and drabs.

A diminutive radiator would hiss randomly for an hour now, a few minutes then, and fall silent too often. The stone walls radiated their own chill so pervasively that she soon knew to avoid any corners where two sides of her would be chilled simultaneously. Her only warmth was found in two unfashionable layers of clothes augmenting the double layer of down comforters tucked tightly beneath her mattress.

She existed on the daily breakfast brought to their room, beginning a lifelong affection for coffee since it was the one warm thing offered, and one other meal, dinner, for which she would deign to leave the hotel, provided it was a restaurant that boasted some form of fire – an oven, a fireplace, whatever.

Between the two events of the day, she read.

She read novel after novel. Like many a hotel in Venice devoted to English-speaking residents, there was a library filled with left novels once cherished by prior residents. All the British classics – Austen, Bronte – plus some of the American ones – Alcott, Howe – suitable for a young lady were made available to her. So, she often found herself upon chilly heaths and in snowy New England, neither of which did anything positive for her mood. Yet she identified with the intense, adolescent brooding of those other women, and how they often had to endure the choices of others.

One of the choices she had to endure was the insistence of her parents that either before or after dinner each day, they would walk, as a family, to a new part of the city. More grey walkways, along green-gray canals crossed by dark bridges, past buildings darkened by coal soot, mold, mildew, and aged. Just to see a pale square with bare trees against a steely sky. Better the walk before with some chance of light rather than the walk afterwards, the cold penetrating her layers and the darkness extreme with most of the residential light locked behind penitential-seeming shutters.

In her travel journal, her comments were routine. "Another grey day in this old lady of a city." "What can I write. Nothing is every new or exciting in this place." "Ate another meal of fish – feel like bait for a whale." "*Death in Venice* was not fiction!"

Yet, in her diary, the one friend she had with her for the journey, another young woman emerged. That young woman was so thrillingly alive, so thoroughly warmed by her nascent sexuality, so immensely enlightened by her connection to heroines of every age, so insightfully challenged by all the questions of existence.

Her writing, thoroughly teenaged in its expressions, was filled with vivid images, colorful illustrations, and lively examples. Sketches of dresses were bright, whimsical, alluring. Short snippets of poetry were filled with rhyming delight. Inside herself, she was so full of life and all of its potential.

On her last day in Venice, she penned this simple entry. "So much to do to be ready for the long train ride tonight. I still have not discovered why so many people have come here. Seems like most of them have come here to die. Nobody seems to come here to live. This place is too small for anyone who is truly alive. I will be so glad to be home. I have felt at odds with this city all my days here."

That afternoon, it snowed gently on an old city that held no allure for her.

Autunno

Why she came back to Venice she was not entirely sure. In the years since her teenage encounter with the city, she had lost too many friends in the war, lost her innocence in the images of concentration camps, lost her coming-of-age in the demands of wartime work, and even lost her scrapbooks and dairies in the many household changes over fifteen years. She had lost so much.

But she had also gained so much. She was now a self - assured young woman in her early thirties with the most wonderful husband in the world, two children (a boy and a girl – thankfully being watched over by her dutiful mother), their own house in the growing suburbs of her hometown. As the president of the Junior Woman's Club, member of the Friends of the Library board, and social chair of her church, her life was both full, fulfilling, and still flowering into even more. The future opened before her, and she liked what she saw on the horizon.

≈≈≈

So much of her earlier days in the city were vague memories. But there was a visceral feeling within her that reminded her that she did not like this place. Yet, here she was. Traveling through Italy on a group tour with her husband and their couples' bridge club. Tony, her best friend's husband, had organized it all, using his own family connections in Florence as a base. The trip over had been far from stuffy on the boat, with the 8 couples, all good friends, finding more than ample ways of partying. The Captain had even saluted their spirit in his last night toast to the passengers. Landing in Naples had meant no long train trips. Their fall trip meant that they enjoyed delightful weather on Capri, and comfortable temperatures in Rome. Yes, the tower leaned in Pisa, David was awesome in Florence, Milan was rebuilding itself stylishly. And now they were heading into Venice across the railroad causeway beneath a declining autumnal sun.

Immediately she felt like nothing had changed. It was still the same old city. But it looked even older. Like an old person, it looked like it had grown shorter, more worn at the edges, more staid in its ways. The hotel confirmed her first impressions – unlike the updated accommodations elsewhere, Venice's hotels looked the same as when she had last been there, only with much wear worn in. Could it be, she wondered, that this was the same hotel she had frozen in the last time? The curtain fabric looked vaguely familiar. She consulted the library and soon found *Little Women* among its works, and there, there on one of the middle pages, were her adolescent words penned in the margins – "If I felt like this, I could live forever."

The same hotel! The same book! And could it be, the same room? She could not tell, but some of the furnishings and even some of the dust beneath the bed could certainly have greeted her in the past.

But she was not the same shivering girl, hiding from

The Venice Stories

the city in her bed. She was now a lively woman, full of life and future. With that mindset she joined the others in their tour of the city. She anticipated the fine seafood, the glorious art, the inviting canals.

As she walked out from the hotel lobby, she was greeted by a single, dry, dead leaf falling from some unseen tree in a declaration of autumn. She brushed it away. She could not as easily brush away the images she began to see as she traveled the city.

Here she saw the falling stucco facade of house after house. There she saw shutters hanging precariously from rusted hinges. Here a walkway to the canal falling away from rot. There a darkened chapel whose art could not be seen for want of a working light. Here an empty restaurant, darkened after the tourist season was over. There a solitary figure of an old woman sitting on a bench, ignored even by the pigeons.

A familiar feeling was creeping into her awareness. She felt at odds with this city. She saw so much ahead, like a perennial plant waiting in the last snows of winter to bloom, while Venice seemed more like an annual giving up its last bit of life before consigning itself into an infinite past.

On their departure a few days later, she did not even look back.

Estate

It had been her own fiftieth birthday gift to herself, but by necessity it was also their twenty-fifth anniversary gift to each other. Of course, they agreed, it would be Italy. It had been decades since they had been there.

Decades filled with children (now thankfully grown and on their own, one presenting them with a precious grandchild), careers (hers as well as his, as her avocations matured into a vocation in management), homes (they had just completed the rehabilitation of their third handyman's special), but few vacations and yet fewer trips and no trips back to Italy. The bridge club had dwindled in the early 60s, and by the late 60s ceased to be. Everyone was too busy finding themselves or losing themselves. More often than not, it was just the two of them at home alone in the evenings, evenings that usually began around 7:30 when each would finally get home. Evenings spent nursing the exhaustion that seemed pandemic in their lives. Weekends, when recovery might be possible, were spent in the routines of maintenance and repair, replacing tired spirits with aching muscles. Weeks slipped into months into years in a seemingly endless cycle of healing either the body or the spirit in rotation. Could they remember their parents living like this, always tired in one way or another?

Finally the weeks were carved from the many schedules. The whole month of July was theirs to share with Italy. But, where to go? In the mode they had adopted in so many things, each of them took on two weeks to plan, and then they would compare what had been penciled in, and in this case duplications would just mean that much more time in a mutually selected region. She had her list easily in mind ... the Ligurian coast, Tuscany, Capri, and then the Amalfi coast. Using her trusted travel agent, she outlined a number of wonderful hotels to accommodate

The Venice Stories

them. With a smile on her face, she presented her husband with her part of the planning. He read it over, and an equal smile appeared on his face. "Ah,", he said, "we will be spending a lot of time in Tuscany and on the two coasts ... they're on my list too." With that he presented her his planned time, and she lost her smile at the last entry.

"Why Venice?" she asked, more sharply than she had intended.

And he patiently spoke about his feeling for the city. When he described Venice, it was not the same city of her memories. His was a city of harmonies, of visual surprises, of continuity and discontinuities, of mystery and profundity. How had she missed all of that?

So, a different smile crept onto her face, the smile of the intrigued partner, not all that sure yet, but willing nonetheless.

The decades had taken their toll more than either of them could have imagined. The itineraries they had planned were suited to their once young bodies, not to their world and work and travel weary frames. Some days they slept in, and missed half a day of sightseeing. Other days they arose on schedule, only to fall to the exhaustion of the day long before the evening events were over. They became some of those American tourists who dine at 6 p.m., because to dine any later would risk falling asleep before the dessert. The adrenaline needed for years of parenting, managing, and maintaining had drained out of them.

One day, in Tuscany, she found herself sitting on the edge of a great broad valley full of lush vegetation, spotting an idyllic farmhouse in the distance that could be had for a song as a permanent Italian retreat. The very thought of such a proposition tired her.

And her husband seemed to fare no better. Mr. Get-up-and-go seemed to have left his energy at the border.

Was this what they faced? A slow slowing until the two of them would become inert objects sitting beside the highway of life? As she thought of this, she realized that life seemed very small to her.

As the train approached Venice, she surprised herself by thinking how nice it would be to find the old hotel, and amid all the faded drapes and musty rooms curl up with a long-forgotten, or was it long-forsaken, book.

Emerging from the train station into the brilliant summer sun, she did not recognize Venice. It was bustling, colorful, full of people. All the young people with their bright clothing ... weren't there only old people here the other times? Buildings with their stucco facades in perfect repair and shutters wide open to a blue sky ... did they tear down the old ones and put these up? The canal sparkling in the sun, alive with the commerce of a modern city ... what was all of this doing here in a dying city?

They took a water taxi to their lodgings, Hotel Moderne; its shining facade a creation of some Milan design house: vibrant, strong, inviting. However, emerging from the stainless steel cage of the elevator, something about the hallway seemed vaguely familiar. She knew, before they turned the corner, where the doors would be. Could it be? But these were doors of smooth laminate, not old splintery wooden ones. Inside the room, she was not sure. The hotel room felt like it had been built yesterday in its similarity to so many hotel rooms she had endured in her work. Yet, when she went to the window and pulled back the sheer, she knew!

It was her old room. Gone were the musty chairs. Gone was the ratty old floor. Gone were the small radiators. But the view was the same, out to a tree that had grown much taller with the passage of the years. And beyond the tree to the campo filled with people sitting and playing and talking, and further still to a canal filled with gondolas and delivery boats.

Venice was vital!

Yet, once again she felt at odds with this city. This time she wanted, no she needed, a sleepy old town in which her sense of age would be welcomed. She wanted it to be OK to be stodgy. She wanted to wrap herself up in some physical representation of memory, and recapture what she had known when she was 16 and when she was 30. Venice would have none of that for her this time.

She asked at the desk about the lending library. The clerk looked perplexed. She explained that in the past the hotel had a room full of left books. The clerk slowly and haltingly explained the hotel had been unused for some years, and when it was again to be opened, everything inside had been disposed of. "It was all too old, and worthless, for the present." She was beginning to know that feeling herself. "And, besides," the clerk added, "with so much to do, few people waste time reading in their rooms," turning to assist a young couple who wanted information about concerts for the evening.

The mid-summer days seemed too long for her. Too much time to be filled, too much warmth to be felt, too many sights to be seen. It felt like Venice had become too full to have a place for her. In this Venice, it felt like life itself was too expansive to have a place for anyone who only wanted to sit the way she did.

On their last night in the city, the great feast of the Redentore, the Guidecca Canal was filled with boats of picnicking friends and families, all awaiting the grand fireworks display. She found that it had no appeal for her. Before the first booming blast had echoed itself into the fabric of the city, she was deep into an exhausted sleep.

Primavera

She had no intention of ever returning to Venice. After all, she was now eighty. At that age, she could make her own choices of what she would and would not do. But she had not counted on the will of the young.

As a gift to her youngest grand daughter, in a tradition she had established with each of the three grandchildren, she offered a trip of choice for spring break in their senior college year.

Almost a decade before, she had spent a strange week at an all-inclusive resort on Jamaica. She doubted she was the kind of single they had in mind, but her eldest grand daughter was perfect material to fulfill any advertising brochure.

A few years after that, granddaughter number two had opted for Iceland. She remembers checking to be sure she had heard correctly, thinking maybe it had been Ireland.

The Venice Stories

However, their tour of geysers, glaciers, and fjords had been delightful, especially in a country where the spring equinox is a national folk holiday.

Before the last grand daughter reached the required point in her academic career, she had begun to travel a different kind of road. Her husband of fifty-two years, with little suffering and less warning, left her alone in the physical world. That would be the hardest journey, she thought.

But when the last of the senior trips was being proposed, and youngest of the lot simply said "Venice,", she knew, somehow, this would be the hardest journey.

Still, her word was her word. They got to choose.

However, curiosity got the better of her, and she had to ask.

"Because it was the place that Grandpa always talked about with me when I was little and wanted a story about some far off land."

She could not control her tears, as she had valiantly done for so long. But she could hide them behind a sudden flurry of busyness.

So, she found herself coming once more to Venice. This trip seemed so removed from that first one, so long ago it seemed to belong to someone else. No long boat trip. No long train trip. This time they flew from New York directly to Venice. This time she approached the city by water, not across the causeway. This time she was coming in spring.

From the dock at Marco Polo airport, she could make out the outline of the city through the slight fog of late morning. As the boat cruised toward Murano, the outline became more of a reality ... she had never seen it arise like this from the sea, like a watery Phoenix waking once more. Circling into San Marco by way of the Lido, she caught the scent of warm spring air.

She had made the arrangements for the hotel, to be sure that she would not end up in the room she had last shared in this city, shared with her husband. This time they were staying in one of those grand hotels on the Grand Canal transformed from a series of Palazzos into a single entity. Elegant, refined, well-tended, well-heated, well-suited for a person of her age and sensibilities. She loved it immediately. Her grand daughter did not.

For a young person the formal lobby was more threatening than imposing. The utter silence of the room and corridors was deafening. The sealed windows kept all the noise, but also the fresh breezes, at bay.

She told her grand daughter to feel free to come and go as she wished. She, herself, was content to spend much of her time in the room, reading and enjoying the view from the window. She was allowed this retreat from Venice for the first two days, but on the third she was confronted in early morning by a very determined young lady. "Grandma," she began, "I didn't come here to be by myself, I came here to be with you. Now get up and get out!" She could have been a drill sergeant!

So, against her deepest feelings, she went out, into a city she thought she knew and which was as foreign to her this time as it had been the time before. The teeming masses of summer tourists were gone, and the breeze was not always totally warming. Much of the modernist edge she had remembered from the last visit had softened with age into a comfortable complement to the antiquity which hid around every bend. But even the antiquities seemed to glow.

She was talked into a concert at Palefenice, the tented opera house that awaits the restoration of the old jewel of the city. She was cajoled into a meal of something other than seafood or liver, finding herself enjoying couscous. She was introduced to neighborhoods she did not know existed by reason of her grand daughter's refusal to use maps. She marveled at a Venice she did not know existed, the Venice of families and children and schools and playgrounds.

After several days of such exploration, she felt done in. All around her, this was a city in bloom, not just by reason of the season, but by reason of its spirit. Had it always been this way?

Once again, she felt at odds with the city. She was looking toward her last days, but this city seemed to be eternally looking to days ahead, even through its ancient eyes. She had little hope for her future, just more travel down the path of loss, while the city seemed to be renewing itself beyond all of its losses. It did not feel like her season in Venice.

On the last night her grand daughter was suddenly invited by some university students to join them for a party. Could she find her way back to the hotel? Of course she could. Go, have fun. All she wanted to do was return to the quiet of the room and drift back in memories, and not memories of Venice.

With the last light of an early spring evening dropping its long shadows down calli and fondamenta, she worked her way through the maze of pathways, using long buried memories to guide her home.

However, before long she sensed she was lost. She needed to ask directions. But where? She turned toward the nearest lit doorway until she looked up to see where she was about to enter. *Hotel Moderne.* Her memories had brought her back once more to the old familiar spot. But her memories also would not let her push open the door. She could not bring herself to enter and ask for directions. O, this city was forever at odds with her!

She felt hopeless, lost. She felt like she was the only person on this pathway. In the distance she could hear the voices of others, jubilantly alive, but that was not her voice. She could smell the warm freshness of spring, but it was not her freshness. In the glass windows of shops she could see the reflections of faces full of joy and hope, but they were not her face.

Suddenly she realized that she was hearing a voice, a very familiar voice, saying very simply, "Come this way." She looked around, but no one seemed to be talking to her. But then the voice came once again, "Come this way," and she followed it. Down a path she would not have chosen, down a path that seemed too dark and cool and old. She heard it again, "Come this way," until she found herself in front of one of those tiny bookstores, crammed full to the rafters. "Come this way," and she entered into the shop, and walked over to the section marked "English Books".

The Venice Stories

The uneven floor tripped her left foot, and she reached out to keep herself from falling. Steadying herself, she looked up at her savior, an old leather bound volume. *Little Women*. She pulled it from its shelf, and it fell open immediately to a page where a teenage girl many years before had written, "If I felt like this, I could live forever."

≈≈≈

And suddenly she remembered what spring really felt like. She bought the book, and with directions from the bookseller, she made her way back to the hotel, stopping to buy a single daffodil to use as a bookmark. And she heard his voice once again, simply saying "Good."

THE ROOM

It was not exactly the kind of present he had planned to give himself.

After all, this was his fiftieth birthday, one of those days of reckoning divisible by ten which usually obligated family and friends to a frenzy of planning to make sure one was suitably distracted from the reality by the inanity and profanity of the gifts offered.

But, business did not allow him the luxury of the party, his attendance being required the day before in Europe. However, even if he had been home, who would have captained such a party? His parents were both dead, he was an only child, he had long since left the town of his birth and childhood, he had never married, and being at the senior level in the firm meant that casual socializing with most of the people of his daily contact would have once seemed been deemed unseemly and now would have been considered either unprofessional or even harassment.

So, he was alone to plan his own celebration of his fiftieth birthday.

And his choice had been to fulfill a long-standing wish ... to see Venice. His business was concluded late on Saturday evening, and he obtained reservations for early Sunday on one of those new high-speed trains that turns

The Venice Stories

Europe into one, albeit sometimes long, commute. He should have been in Venice before noon, with a full afternoon and evening to explore *The Jewel of the Adriatic* before catching a connecting flight to his already scheduled flight home on Monday morning. Yes, he knew, it was only one day. Yes, he knew people spent weeks, months, years, and even lifetimes exploring the city. And, yes, even a day in Venice would be a better way to spend his birthday than on a plane or at a business hotel in the middle of nowhere near some airport in Europe.

Well, that had been the plan anyway.

He had not figured on the perversity of the railway unions of Europe, and their propensity for expanding the Easter holidays by days or weeks in advance through "job actions." Hell, it was a strike! And as a strike, it was hell!

The high-speed first class train became a crowded conventional train of indiscriminate class, which rumbled across borders on a schedule known to no one. Stops were unpredictable, delays at connecting stations indeterminate, food service non-existent. When he finally stumbled off the train about 9 pm in Venice's St. Lucia station, filled with more railway terminal sandwiches and beverages than he had ever wanted to consume (he felt he had finally discovered the meaning "terminal" in the description of such places), he only desired to get to his hotel, maybe have some warm food, a shower, and a long sleep.

He had also not figured on the perversity of hotel hyperbole either. The high quality hotel that boasted of recent renovations and luxurious accommodations on its website must have held different understandings of words like "quality", "renovations", and "luxurious". But, the room was clean, the bed comfortable, the bathroom adequate, and the restaurant open.

He treated himself to a pitcher of prosecco to toast his own birth, accompanying the bubbles with some quite wonderful seafood; well, actually the seafood had initially tasted ordinary but rose in estimation as the wine lowered in the pitcher. By the time he finished café and dolce, he was not seeing the day as a total loss. True, all he had seen of Venice was a short canal ride to his hotel, and in the morning he expected to see even less on his way to the airport at too early an hour. So he contented himself with the prospect of a good night's sleep. How long had it been since he had truly had a good night's sleep. He could not remember.

In his room, he completed his evening rituals – unpacking his clothes for the next day, a warm shower and appropriate time for other matters of the bathroom, placing his travel clock on the bedside table with the alarm set. Then, with a sigh, he switched off his light, and entered the deep darkness which is a Venice room when the shutters are closed.

He quickly drifted off into a drowsy sleep without consciousness or dream. After a period of time he could not determine, he was summoned back to the surface of consciousness from the depths of delights by some sound. It was coming from the room adjoining his room, the one toward his bathroom.

At first he was not sure that he really heard anything.

The Venice Stories

Then he heard it again. It was the sound of a child, a girl, calling softly but plaintively for her parents. "Mommy, Daddy, I need you." However, there was an edge to the words that evoked deep emotions in him. Between the words he now heard the small sounds of sobs. Then the words again, this time a little louder. "Oh," he thought, "won't someone comfort the child." Even as he thought this, he wondered where these deeply empathetic thoughts came from. He had never had a child. He rarely spent time with children. His only experience of children was from having been one. That was decades ago, as this day proved.

Yet, the longing of his heart for some kind of peace for this child was profound. He felt like he ached inside, and wished someone would come to her side, her aid, her comfort.

The small voice on the other side of the wall, in broken sentences between sighs and sobs, continued for what seemed an eternity until, at last, a door more distant opened and two adult voices joined the girl's. He could not make out the full conversation, a mix of adult reassurances and youthful concern and relief. "...OK...", "...nothing wrong...", "...woman now..." and suddenly he felt himself burning with embarrassment. He had been unknowingly privy to one of the most significant moments in some unknown girl's life. The universe had open for a moment, and allowed him a glimpse into a world he thought was closed to him, the intimate relationships of parent and child, child and adult, men and women. Now he heard the sound of quiet laughter coming from the adjoining room, and then the closing of that distant door, and then silence.

In the dark silence of his room, he merged back into the depths.

Again he was roused toward consciousness by a sound. This time it came from the room above him. It was the sound of something large being dropped or thrown to the floor, or at least that is how it sounded to him below it. Then, following a short moment of silence, raised voices in some language other than his own. Still, he could tell they were angry voices. A man and a woman. Both angry. Shooting words at each other. And then the sound of a slap. There was no mistaking the sound. And the cry of pain ... but he could not tell if the painful cry was male or female. And then the sound of more flesh contacting flesh, and that sound of something going to the floor, and this time he knew it was the sound of someone's body hitting the floor. But whose? The words continued to be thrown about, and they now had the ring of tears at their edge. This was all above and beyond him. He was a meek man, never one to enjoy the roughhouse of youth, the prize fights of young adults, or violence of any kind. What should he do? What could he do? Wasn't there anyone who could stop this? And then, just as suddenly, he heard the door above slam, and a heavy tread disappear slowly down the upper hallway. An eerie silence took hold of his room, and he found himself holding his breath. This all had happened in the space of less than a minute, but it seemed an eternity. How much longer would he have to endure waiting, not knowing what had happened above? But then, equally suddenly, he heard another slam of the door, and an equally heavy tread disappear down the

The Venice Stories

upper hallway, but this time the feet were running, as if trying to catch up to someone or something. He had been an unwitting party to another of life's private moments, those times of hidden violence when power and love get mixed in ways that he could not fathom or understand. It made him physically ill to the same degree that the first awakening had left him feeling honored and almost faint. This time, his return to sleep did not come easily, as the scene imagined through the sounds played again and again in his mind, the characters and plot changing with each rehearsal. Eventually the physical and emotional exhaustion of it all captured him back into sleep.

"Damn these thin walls," he said to himself when he was roused once more from sleep. "What is it this time?"

This time it was from the room beneath him. Two men were talking. Their voices were gentle, no violence in their tones at all. Just quiet talking, with some long pauses at times. Then, he heard the quiet notes of music, as if from a radio. He began to hear the slightest sound of feet rhythmically shuffling their way into dance. The voices spoke less, and softer now, and the gentleness of their tone deepened to the point where it was almost like hearing whispers meant only for the two of them. And then the music ended, a toilet downstairs flushed twice, a bed groaned, and groaned some more, and the two voices seemed to say good night to each other. It was all so loving, so inviting, so caring, so gentle, that he found himself saying "good night" to the room below as if he were one of the men ... and in his drift into sleep he became aware, surprisingly without anxiety, that the universe had opened one more of its intimate secrets, one he would not have opened for himself.

The clock read 3:37 when he looked at it ... and now the sound was coming from the room across the small airshaft outside one of his windows. It was the sound of someone singing softly. A woman's voice. A voice that was like joy itself. He could not make out the words, for it was more vocalization than a song. Sometimes a humming, sometimes more, it rose in pitch and tempo to a seeming ending only to wrap itself in a new melodic line ready to grow again. This was not a practice session. This was a person and a song becoming one, song expressing life, and life embodying song, or so it seemed to him. He had never heard anything so beautiful in his whole life. For all of his tours of galleries, all of his attendance at concerts, all of his reading of books, nothing in art had every touched him like this sound. He found that he was crying soft tears of joy, just from the sound of this song. He did not want the song to end. He wanted to be lullabied by that song into eternity. To its strains he drifted back into a sleep in which he dreamt not in images or words, but of that song. Ah ...

Aw ... this was no song. This was noise! This was, wait, he knew that sound. Full of energy and breathing and skin. And then the rhythmic junction of two voices, rising in intensity until one yelped and the other moaned. Then silence. It was from the room at the head of his bed. And then it began again. Slowly, then reaching more fevered tones, to a climax as heated as the first one. Then, a longer silence ("thank goodness"), but it began once more, even more slowly, but with a persistent energy that seemed like

The Venice Stories

it would overwhelm his room too. "What are they, animals?" he wondered, but then noticed his own libido had been stoked into a firmness he had not felt in many a year. Another intimate glimpse into the lives of others which also opened a glimpse into his own live, his own emotions, his own horniness. And were they really beginning again in the next room? Could they be? He heard a moan of deep passion, and only slowly realized that it was his own. In the echo of his own identification with the neighboring activities, he drifted back into sleep, the kind of sleep that usually only follows one's complete union with someone other than self.

He awoke with a great start. In the deep blackness he thought he must have heard a sound, but all was stillness. Utter stillness, and suddenly he had that experience of not knowing where he was. Nothing about him was familiar. He felt adrift in the universe, not anchored to any place, any personality. He was terrified. He did not know where he belonged. He felt his heart racing, his body quickly perspiring, his breathing becoming labored. He tried to use his mind to place himself, but he could not remember where he had gone to sleep. This was not a place with which he was familiar. He fumbled around him for something familiar, and finally found the light switch. The first flash of light more disoriented him than oriented him. This was a strange room. He still did not know where he was. But slowly, in the back of his mind, he was beginning to know. Yet, it was only with a frantic opening of the shutter on the one true window in the room, yielding view of the side canal, that he fully remembered. He was in

Venice. But as anchored as he became in that spot, he still felt adrift. Something felt changed, something felt unfamiliar, in the person he was knowing as himself. It was disconcerting. He touched his clothes, he went into the bathroom and looked at and touched his toothbrush and razor. They all seemed familiar yet not as familiar as they had once seemed. He urinated into the toilet, and assured himself he was still very physical, and all the parts were working as they should. It was only his mind that was different ... or that his mind was reflecting something else that was different. It was a mind, but he could not be totally sure it was his, at least did not belong to the "him" who had endured a hellish train trip, a mediocre dinner, and a night of interrupted sleep. The "him" he could now think about seemed deeper and wider than he had ever been, or allowed himself to be. He was frightened. He was afraid he was not only losing it, but that he had lost "it", some unnamed thing that made him "him".

And then he heard a sound. It was the sound of another toilet flushing somewhere near him, in one of the other rooms. And a few moments later, in another room, he could hear a shower being started. It was just like so many other days of his life, on the road, in his condo, wherever. Life was going on, he would still be himself, it was OK. He could feel himself relax. The sounds of life around him assured him that nothing had changed. Through the open shutters, he could make out the dim glow on the sky that heralded the day's start as it had started for nearly fifteen hundred years in this city of reeds, water, islands, people, travelers, hotels, and rooms.

The Venice Stories

≈≈≈

He slowly shaved, showered, dressed, repacked, and then took his cappuccino in the room. At 6:20 am, right on his pre-arranged schedule, he walked down the stairs from his room, ready to check out, catch his 6:25am water taxi to the airport, and make his 7:35 flight to Milano. At the desk, he returned his key and signed the credit card slip. The clerk, a pleasant young woman in her twenties, asked him if he had enjoyed a good night. "Hardly," he replied curtly, turning to leave. She quickly responded, "O, I'm sorry to hear that. I thought you would have had an especially good night, since you were our only guest in that wing of the hotel." He stopped, and then heard her add, "and, Signore, it was your birthday!" He turned around, but found he was alone in the lobby.

THE LOVERS

All of this really happened! I swear.
    I should know. I was there that night.
And lest you think that I was mistaken because it was dark, this was one of those wonderful, first quarter moon nights, when the early evening was lighted hauntingly.

And lest you think that I was perhaps, how shall I say this, under the influence, I had only had one small glass of prosecco as my *umbra*, nothing more.

And lest you think that I could have no way of knowing what was going on in the minds of these people, you are right ... but then I think I do, and I think you do too.

It was a late spring night when, having shopped for a gift near San Marco, according to my habit of never, ever going into a shop which translates its welcome into more than two languages, I made my way home along my habitual path. I expected a most ordinary stroll, but I was very much mistaken.

After a final look at the Basilica in the last rays of the sunset and the first bath of moonlight, I exited Piazza San Marco by that route which skirts the edges of the inland gondola lagoon. You know the place, I am sure.

Coming to my first bridge, the one over the Rio dei Fuseri, I stopped back a short ways, for on the top of the

The Venice Stories

bridge was a young woman dressed fully in white. Standing there all alone at the bridge's peak, she looked like she was posing for some advertisement, and I quickly looked about for the photographer. But, this was no photo shoot, and I soon saw that she was looking in both directions with an intense eagerness, a hopeful yet anxious gaze. I moved to the shadows to see how this drama would play out.

Several times distant footsteps echoed under arcades and along fondamente, and I was nearly as intent as this woman in white to see who was approaching. The parade of comings and going contained the usual assortment: business people still heading home after too-late office hours, seemingly lost tourists full of maps and backpacks, young Venetians with cell phones glued to their heads, and some gondoliers beginning their evening shifts.

I had nearly given up my own hope for a resolution when a softer tread was heard from the far side of the bridge, and my white apparition gave out an audible sigh. Arms raised in greeting, she went down the other side to connect with the arrival, and by her almost cooing, I knew this was a greeting of love. But, I was not to see the greeting, so I restarted on my way, feeling more than a little disappointed at not receiving the satisfaction of seeing the reunion. Imagine my joy as I ascended the bridge to see the head and then shoulders of my friend-in-white coming the other way, now linked by arms behind each other with her awaited. O, such love flowed between them; I almost blushed at being a witness to this time of intimacy. Then the two women descended toward San

Marco, and I was on my way, happily rejoicing that the evening had so wonderfully shared its romance with me.

≈≈≈

Twisting through the area between San Marco and the Rialto, I enjoyed the many sights in the shop windows until I reached San Salvador Bridge, but was stopped again before I crossed. This time it was by a crowd of school children on one of those trips to Venice, probably on their way back to San Marco after a dinner of pizza somewhere. Once they had ceased to occupy the whole bridge, I was about to cross when I saw that some of them, well actually only two of them, had not yet left. I paused just a moment, looking up from the shadows towards these two illuminated by the moonlight. They looked to be in their early teens, and o, so young, and o, so innocent, and o, so awkward. And then, in a moment of grace, two young hands touched the parapet together, and two young faces moved silently toward each other, and two sets of young lips met for just a moment, and two sets of young eyes locked upon each other, and then two awkward youths looked away, and she first and he following, quickly ran to catch up with the noisy herd evident in the distance. And all I could do was stand there, caught up for a few moments in the emotions of that place, that time, those youth, that love.

≈≈≈

The Rialto was busy, as always. People standing, people going this way or that, and some people seemingly going this way *and* that. As exciting as I find arriving there, I find departing its bright clutch and hustle a

The Venice Stories

challenge. Down the narrow passage, approaching the Rio di Fontego, the crowds always pinch in a bit. So, we all were moving slowly along, kept gradual in our progress by the slowest window-shoppers ahead. I became aware that the couple behind me were upset, however it took me a while to understand that they were not upset by the slowness of the traffic but by each other. They were speaking in those expressively quiet tones which communicated so well their great anger with each other. As we began to inch along towards the bridge their voices began to rise and become clipped in cadence. I could almost feel a chill go down my spine, the coldness behind me was so apparent. It became all the more so when with an "OK, don't!" the irate conversation ended. In that icy silence we all began the climb over the bridge, and the reason for the undue slowness of the crowd became apparent; to our left the moon was playing tricks on the waters of the Grand Canal like some elfin magician. I glanced at it, warmed by the view, and then gave my full attention to the diagonal crossing of the bridge and the steps down until I heard a voice, so recently full of venom, now say wistfully "Dear, look at that!" which was answered by an equally loving "O, my, what a sight." Glancing back in my slight turn onto the downward treads, I saw one hand caringly engage another hand, and a soft breeze of summer warmth seemed to fill the air.

≈ ≈ ≈

I always stop at the bridge over the Rio dei San Giovanni, because the toy store there fascinates me. Windows of plush animals, puzzles, games, models, and so much more. Actually, what fascinates me are the children who stand in front of the windows, making their wishes hopefully known to any willing and able adult.

Tonight several such children were noisily asserting their choices until they were called to move on, and I was suddenly left with only two other people in front of the windows. There was no mistaking them as a couple – they held hands, and spoke in the gentle whispers of a shared conspiracy of love. Yet, I could not understand their deep fascination with the windows. Behind them was a much more awesome sight of the canal bathed in that magic light, a gondola softly gliding beneath. Still, the windows held their attention. They inspected each one at length, pointing at this, talking about that. And then with a quick hug, they turned to leave, and I saw that in probably one or two months theoretical toys would have a more practical role in their life as new parents. They walked away, slowly, still speaking gently to each other.

≈≈≈

From there the way twists and turns, into the small corte, through the narrow passageway, under the arcade, leading to the abrupt bridge of Santa Apostoli. It was with relief that I found no crowds ahead. No jostling in the narrow part, an ability to see where (and into what) I was stepping – it was wonderful. Up, over the bridge, past the young man standing by the rail, holding one of those roses sold by itinerants in the restaurants and on the streets. He looked sad, very sad. He was holding the rose, fidgeting with some of the bottom leaves, peeling them away to drop on the bridge. I was already down the bridge when I heard

The Venice Stories

the small splash behind me, and then the footsteps coming down the bridge behind me. The young man reached me just as I was about to turn the corner onto the Strada Nova, his hands sunk deeply into his pockets, his head hanging down, and a look on the portion of his face I could see that would tear at the heart of anyone who had ever loved. Even as the echo of his now shuffling steps faded in the distant *calle* he had taken, I could feel his anguish.

≈≈≈

I moved down the Strada Nova more slowly now. I felt personally shaken, like a piece of my soul had also been taken. The wider path, usually a pleasure, seemed painfully lonesome this evening. As a person would approach me, I would scan her or his face, trying to decide if they were about to break a heart or suffer a broken heart.

In time, I could see the Chiesa de San Felice on the other side of the broad bridge honoring the same pleasant saint. Ahead of me was a single couple making their way up the bridge, going in the same direction as I was. I knew who they were immediately. He, in his usual felt hat with jaunty feather, tie with stick pin, sport coat with lapel label of some cause, pants with crisp crease, shoes shined to a mirror polish, and the silver handled cane held by his ringed fingers. She, with a typically bright scarf on her head, a dress suit of dark blue wool, gold jewelry at ears, neck, and wrists, dark hose leading into matching blue shoes as polished as his, and her ringed hand holding firmly on his free arm. I estimated that each of them had crossed these bridges for more than eight decades, probably once at a racing pace, then at a more business-like gait, then at the leisurely rate of the retired, and now at the careful cadence of age.

They moved as a unit, a motion beginning in one finding its completion in the other. First one of his feet would rise a step, and she would flow behind to the same step. Then her rocking motion of bringing both her feet to the new step would swing his trailing foot to that step, before the other foot would reach again for the next step. It was like they were dancing a very, very gradual dance, *ala* a slowed down Fred and Ginger, across the bridge. I wondered how either of them would have the freedom of the city if not for the many types of companionship given by the other. As I passed them, I offered a quiet *buona sera*, but they did not seem to hear me, perhaps for lack of youthful hearing, or more likely because they were so intent on each other that I could not penetrate their affection.

≈≈≈

He walked past me almost as soon as I descended to the front of San Felice. Young, well maybe not that young, but dressed in all the current styles, smelling sweetly of just a right amount of cologne. He walked with a clean, eager step. And then, suddenly, his pace quickened, and with an obviously joyful shout of *Caio Massimo*, he almost ran to the top of the Ponte di Noale, into the welcoming arms of an equally excited, equally well-dressed man. Hugs gave way to a long, passionate kiss, finally broken by a passerby's sarcastic whistle. Then, with a shared laugh, the two were off, hand in hand, toward the train station

The Venice Stories

and out of my sight. By the time I reached that same point on the bridge, all that remained was a lingering, mingling scent of well-matched colognes.

≈≈≈

There, on the other side of the bridge, is the shop where I bought my hairbrush. And here, still open, the stand that sells the hot wine in the winter. The old, preserved Farmacia stands alongside the modern equivalent. The turn to the right through the *campo* heads deep into Cannaregio, but I continued straight on.

I found that my mind was so full of all the emotions I had witnessed and experienced, I was gradually becoming oblivious to my surroundings, or so I thought. Maybe it was only the extraneous material goods I stopped noticing, for I very clearly saw the two of them ahead of me at the diagonal steps of the bridge at the Maddalena. I took them for mother and son, their ages obvious in their clothes, their faces, their demeanor. That is, I took them for mother and son until he stopped her at the top of the bridge, leaned in to her face, and started a kiss of obvious passion, as sexual as any I have ever had or dreamed about. She leaned into his body, wrapping an arm around him in a provocative fashion, and allowed one leg to rise strokingly against his.

I felt my own breath taken away, my pulse racing a bit, almost like I was a party to this encounter between the generations, but I could not sense whether I longed to be the younger or the older lover.

I was jarred from my revelry by their passage past me, their amorous aura like flame warming me.

≈≈≈

By then, the evening's chill offered little warmth when the radiance of that moment wore off, and so I moved on, hoping my exertion would warm me as thoroughly as had their passion.

My pace quickened, and I began to feel less chilled, passing that shop where I have bought shoes, and up toward the narrow crossing of the Rio di San Marcuola. I was again walking against the stream of pedestrians who were making their way from the train station towards, well towards who-knows-where. Wheeling their suitcases behind them, they were more like a giant Saharan camel caravan than a flow of humans. Heads down, grunts of burden, linear progress, they flowed up and down the bridge, appearing to be stranger following stranger.

Or, at least I took them all to be strangers. Especially the two I saw as we approached the top of the stairs from opposite directions. One was as luxuriantly dark as any mahogany, the other as blondly light as a sunny noon. Yet, against all my pre-conceptions, the two paused as I passed, and with a quick smile and an exchange of a larger bag for a smaller one, they gave their lips a brief intimacy, and then wordlessly moved on, now, to my enlightened eyes, obviously a couple ... a couple of a lovingly changing world.

≈≈≈

The street market was just closing itself as I passed along the Rio Terre San Leonardo. The tourist restaurants poured out the first shift of those who insist on eating at a very un-Italian six, and welcomed in the first of those

The Venice Stories

more acclimated to a later dinner. Ahead was my turn to the right, along the Cannaregio Canal, no more bridges to cross, and I could not tell if this relieved or disappointed me, given the events of my evening so far.

Ahead of me the pointed guards of the bridge bearing their name, Guglie, warned me of the few steps I would need to maneuver even though I would not be crossing the bridge. I chose the left-hand path, because this would put me on the more gentle ramped ascent and descent. As I made my way through the crowd, I found myself stopped for just a moment at the point where I needed to turn right. But that moment was enough to overhear the conversation of two young people stopped by the rail of the bridge. She asked simply, "Wo ist der Bahnhof?" in search of the train station. And he replied, "Non capisco," registering his lack of understanding. I then heard an English request for the station replied to with a French lack of understanding. But, by then the crowd was breaking, and I had to move on. At the end of the ramp, I moved slightly canalward, and turned to see if I could witness the conclusion of this small drama. They were still there, lips still alternately moving, but no appearance of understanding on either's part. Then slowly, gently, I saw her hand reach up his arm and grip his bicep ever so slightly. His head, by a hint of a nod, acknowledged her touch. The words seemed to have stopped replaced by a shared gaze. Then his hand, just as slowly, even more gently, rose up, and turned to stroke her hair, and then the side of her cheek. They were both smiling. Her free hand joined his at her face, but she did not take his away. She briefly held it against her cheek, and then slowly transferred it to her lips. He reciprocated by moving her hand to his lips. Then, without a word, the two of them, now hand-in-hand, turned and walked away ... and not towards the station. An audible *Ah* passed my lips, causing some near me to look at me in wonder, which was exactly the same state I was in.

≈≈≈

And now, at last, my own neighborhood. The household goods store, the wine shop with its giant jugs, and ahead my grocers'. And in the distance, the bridge of *Tre Archi* loomed, and beyond it my own home. Walking along the familiar stones, I greeted the black cat who lives in the barred window, who meowed in response.

Looking up at the bridge, as I do each time I go by it, I was startled to see a single figure near its top, looking out on the canal with a deep longing. At first I thought I was seeing myself, waiting there to present the gifts I had purchased in San Marco to my beloved, waiting for a loving embrace, longing for a passionate kiss. Then I saw the smile that lights my world coming over the bridge, looking straight at me, and not at the other person at all. This lover was mine!

≈≈≈

So, looking more closely at the stranger on the bridge, I realized it was you.

Or was that you on one of the other bridges?

THE JOURNEY

The Departure

It was just one of those perfect days that occur now and then in one's life.

Not that any one feature of the day was perfect, but in the totality perfection seemed poised.

He had just enjoyed the best trans-Atlantic flight in his memory. Boarding at JFK had been a breeze, the plane left the gate early and they were immediately "first in line for takeoff", the plane was pleasantly full but not crowded, so many were seasoned travelers that the flight attendants served dinner to the few who wanted it quietly and without a fully lit cabin, and so he had gotten nearly 7 hours of good sleep. In the morning, he had awakened to the smell of hot coffee and the announcement that they would be arriving into Marco Polo Airport 35 minutes early. When the pilot had thanked everyone for flying with them, he had even thought to himself in response to the pilot, "And thanks for getting us here."

But the flight was only one piece of the puzzle.

His destination was another piece. Venice was one of those destinations which, in his mind, a person welcomed no matter what the circumstances.

And his circumstances were yet another piece.

The Venice Stories

Five years of hard work in the burgeoning Internet field had provided him with sufficient stock options that he could leave all that work behind and do whatever he wanted. He was one of the lucky few who started early enough to get out early enough to truly benefit from those benefits. He came to Venice not on work, but on desire.

The sunny morning seemed like icing on his cake.

In his jubilant mood, he found the baggage collection as well as the immigration and customs process more pleasant than annoying. So, with his life before him, full of promise and hope and joy, he exited the terminal and walked over to the waterbus dock to await the next boat to San Marco.

The sun was nicely warm on his face. The sea had that deliciously sweet smell of salt, seaweed, and fish. The light breeze gently tossed his hair about in a way that reminded him of his youth.

Around him he could hear conversations in many different languages, some singsong, some more guttural, some seemingly without interruptions between words. Even the conversations going on in English sounded exotic to him.

As he waited, he turned to look at the cars passing behind him on the roadway to the terminal, and was surprised to catch sight of himself reflected in the glass of an advertising kiosk. He was that smiling, childlike person widely grinning back at him. Wow!

The time passed quicker than he ever remembered and the golden Alilaguna boat was nearing the dock. He joined the small group that slowly ambled forward toward the landing area.

The rope was fastened to the stanchion, the boat's gangway opened, and out came a mass of people. But what a mass. A hurrying crowd, full of grim faces, sharp tongues, jostled baggage.

Who were these people? Where did they come from? He could not understand it. They were in the most magical city in the world, on a day of breeze and sun, with the shining sea their companion. How could they not notice?

But soon they were gone, and his arrival group on their way toward Murano, the Lido, and San Marco. Cameras clicked. Fingers pointed. Voices *oooe*d and *ahhh*ed. Even those with Italian as their native tongue were speaking of the scenery and not business. Only one or two were glued to their cell phones.

After checking into his hotel, he took his first walk. As always he was amazed not only by the glimpse of familiar sights but also by the glimpse of new sights. Was there no end to delights to be found in this tiny jewel-box of a city?

Apparently not.

His first month was spent settling in. Yes, there were meetings with lawyers and notaries and banks. Details beyond belief to be dealt with, but he felt Venetian time settling in. As busy as any day might become, at 12:30 or 1pm the day would be broken by a meal, a leisurely conversation, a walk, time on a bench on some Fondamente, or some other soul-feeding activity. Business might resume at 3 or 4pm, if at all.

Surprisingly, by the end of the month, without a single frantic day, everything that needed to be done, was done.

The Venice Stories

It was as if time were elastic.

In Venice, time would often seem elastic. Days would leak into weeks, yet each would have its own quality. Evenings began not by time on watches but by shared activities with others. Sometimes it began over a pre-opera drink. Sometimes it began with a concert. Sometimes it began with a late supper at 10pm. Days with busy agendas seemed to last long enough to be fulfilled, against all logical odds. Anticipated events came along without delay or anxiety. Time was acting as fluid as the major medium of the city.

But it was not only time that began to take on this quality.

Light had the ability to bend corners in Venice. Seeing a shaft of light was not always a clue as to where the sun could be glimpsed down a narrow calla. Windows facing north seemed to have more light streaming into them than anywhere else in the northern hemisphere. At sunset, the eastern sky was often as deep painted as the western sky. And such a fluid light interacted playfully with the buildings and the canals to make shadows dance and darkness glow and dimensions appear and disappear.

Space without skyscrapers, but also without the broad vistas of the big sky country, measured itself differently. On days of sunshine it stretched itself long, from the distant Dolomites to the embracing Lido. On days of fog it barely stretched itself at all, choosing instead to be measured in feet, in steps. Even on the days between the two extremes, space varied depending on where you were amid the islands. Tight calli would press in, making it long and narrow. Grand campi would open out, making it wide and tall. Some buildings with long windows invited space to grow upward. Some with porticos and arcades would seem to trap it within. It often felt like even an infinite team of surveyors could never plot the city.

Sounds, from the gentle rip-rip-rapping of the smallest wave on the canal walls to the summoning clanging of the biggest bells in the tallest towers, held their own definition as well. It was never and yet always surprising to be amid sound, even noise, and take a simple corner and find complete, absolute silence. Above the strains of everyday life, one might catch a phrase of music from some window, but where? Or maybe a distant call of a marketeer, haggling over sepia, but where? A mother and daughter, in agreement or argument (who could say?) echoing beyond sight, but where? And then nightfall would come, and with it a greater depth of silence and a deeper clarity of sounds. Walking down a deserted walkway, way past midnight, one could become aware just how loud the sound of heels and soles are on pavement when it is the only sound.

Life, in its comings and goings, was changed as well. Each new child in a neighborhood found a universal and expressed welcome as the new keepers of a way of life slowly disappearing into history. Each death was announced by notices complete with color photos (since sometimes names were not enough in a world where friendliness often preceded acquaintance), posted where all the passersby could see the vagary of existence. And then there were the boat processions to the island of San

The Venice Stories

Michele, to commit a body to permanent residence in Venice.

In between those two events, life expresses itself uniquely as well. A strange mix of daring and acceptance sustains a people who learn to live a grand life in the most unlikely of settings. Buildings have risen up, generations have lived in them. Tides have come and gone, floods sometimes riding on their backs. Plagues have ravaged, and enterprises have flourished. Yet through all these material manifestations, of humanity and nature, the only constant has been life: the life of the islands, the life of the lagoon, the life of the sea, and the life of the people of the islands, the lagoon, the sea. Few people are reminded as frequently by their location how connected they are to their own history.

And even spirit, the ephemeral existence beyond matter and life, has an existence all its own in the hallowed and seemingly holy place. Even the most callous nonbeliever senses something more inclusive than the moment amid the churches and the canals. Those with more openness to the power of that which is unseen sense its presence permeated into the very web of all existence in Venice. Is there even one place to sleep, wake, eat, work, sit, walk, worship, enjoy, and sleep again which has not served the same purpose for many others in the past? Restoration, the perennial activity of the city, often strips away a veneer of three or four centuries only to discover a layer already old when first covered. One senses that one is not the only one to have passed this way. The connection to spirit seems most palatable more often than not.

Randolph W.B. Becker

One is not just alive, but alive in connection to an existence which transcends all the usual concepts of time, space, light, and sound.

By the second month, he had begun his deeper exploration into this phenomenon of life within the walls of a city with walls of water. He lost track of how long this process was taking. Many months later he startled himself when he said, in response to an inquiry about his status, "O, I've only just gotten here." He felt like he was constantly arriving, coming anew into a new city renewed with each rising of sun and moon.

He would greet these newly arrived days much as he had at the Aeroporto. He would find his own face among the reflected images of a shop window, and see that once again he was grinning.

He became a tour guide of sorts to many of his friends. They would arrive at his doorstep ready to experience history, art, architecture, music, theater, and literature, and he would disappoint all those expectations by offering up joy. No one ever left his company feeling cheated by the trade. He invited others to move beyond the time of clock and watch, by being slave to neither. He taught people how to sit and try to measure the changing light of a sun setting behind Salute, by the simple act of sitting. He tutored friends in the art of listening to silence, often by saying nothing. He advised visitors to follow routes which would surely get them lost, that they might find themselves. He helped the uncertain to feel the spirit of the city, by offering up accounts of his own spiritual experiences.

Then one day in the second year in his paradise, the

The Venice Stories

letter came. Just a mention among other items from his brother. This, like all things of the "other" world, would pass.

Several months later, the mention had become a concern.

And in several more months, the concern had become a crisis.

And in the beginning of the third year, the crisis had become a responsibility.

A responsibility to which he needed to respond.

So it was that on a bright, very sunny day, with only a hint of a breeze, he boarded the Alilaguna waterbus at San Marco to take him to Marco Polo airport. He did not notice that almost no one was looking out of the boat as it passed between the islands. Many of the travelers were glued to their cell phones, transacting frantic last minute business. Only one camera clicked, and that by a tourist taking a photo of her husband against the backdrop of the city that was fast retreating into memory. Neither the city nor the husband seemed to smile for the photo. He barely noticed, being more focused on the schedule of his flights, the details of his leaving, the many more details that awaited him. His mind raced through the contents of his suitcases to assure himself he had not forgotten anything.

As the boat slowed to dock, he pushed forward like all of the rest to gather up luggage and prepare to disembark. Once the gangway was opened he was part of the hurrying crowd, full of grim faces, sharp tongues, jostled baggage. Yet on the dock people stood randomly about, seemingly with no sense of direction or purposes, talking and laughing, smiling like idiots.

Who were these people? Where did they come from? He could not understand it. How could they be so happy, so aimless at a time like this?

Ahead of him he saw a man who looked vaguely familiar, a man of seriousness and busyness, a man who knew the measures of time and space, the oppressions of darkness and noise, the limitations of life and spirit. And then he recognized his own reflection in the glass of an advertising kiosk.

Suddenly, he felt like Adam, fleeing out through the gates of his own Eden.

The Arrival

It was just one of those awful days that occur now and then in one's life.

Not that any one feature of the day was awful, but in the totality imperfection seemed poised.

He had just enjoyed the worst trans-Atlantic flight in his memory. Instead of a direct flight, he had to endure one of those short hops in Europe to a bustling hub-city whose airport had been built for half the crowd it was now experiencing. Delayed connecting planes delayed his main flight, which then inched its way skyward for half an hour on backed-up taxiways. The plane was so full that even his business class seat seemed crammed with the journeys of too many others. Being a day flight, the welcomed respite of a night's sleep was lost, replaced instead with bright lights, noisy service, mediocre meals, and streaming entertainment watched by people who at home would never have watched the same things. In the late afternoon, filled with too much coffee and too many sweets, he endured the announcement that they would be circling New York for about half an hour. When the pilot had apologized for the delay, he had thought to himself in response to the pilot, "And thanks for nothing."

But the flight was only one piece of the puzzle.

His destination was another piece. Coming back to the States meant coming back to clogged expressways, honking horns, and larger-than-life but smaller-than-meaningful community identity.

And his circumstances were yet another piece.

He had returned from a very early retirement, recalled to a life he had thought was over forever. Even though he possessed the wealth that made his Venice life possible, such wealth does not ensure freedom, especially freedom from responsibility and feelings.

He came back from Venice not on desire, but on duty.

The rainy late afternoon seemed like the last straw.

At curb side, the dampness of the day coupled with the fumes of too many vehicles until he thought he would suffocate. Even if it had been sunny, the protective architecture would have kept him far from direct rays. The chilling breeze outside whistled aggressively through the tunnel like arrival area. All around him English was being yelled like some form of weapon.

As he waited for the shared limo that would take him to the house, he turned to look at the cars passing behind him on the roadway directly in front of the terminal, and was surprised catching sight of himself reflected in the glass of an advertising kiosk. He looked like death itself, a shadow of a real person, oddly without identifying emotion, barely any eyes or mouth to be seen, like someone in the process of disappearing.

His first month was spent settling in. There were meetings with lawyers and notaries and banks. Details beyond belief to be dealt with, and he felt the old pace settling in. Begun at 9am, a day would stretch to 6 or even 9 pm without much break.

In a passage of time that seemed more empty than full, the concern that had become crisis that had become responsibility became loss. He had known loss before, but this time it hit him harder than before, or was it that he allowed it to hit him harder than before.

Yet, when the appropriate number of days had passed, or least what others told him were the appropriate number of days, he took on both the family's business and the family business. Without the time and space and energy and spirit to look back, he plunged deep into the future. So many counted on him now.

And Venice seemed so far away, so long ago, so other worldly.

He did not notice that spring had come and was in full bloom. One day, driving himself into the headquarters, still struggling to regain the comfort with driving he had lost in those years of walks and boats, he felt a vaguely familiar sensation in the steering wheel. Something instinctual told him to pull over. When he did and inspected the car, he saw the right rear tire was flat. His

The Venice Stories

every-ready cell phone made easy work of summoning the roadside assistance service, who vowed to be there within the hour. "Within the hour!" he cursed, as he kicked the tire. But, just as he was reaching for his briefcase to use the time to read some reports, a far distant sound caught his ear. It was a bell, a church bell. From the highway he could not see where, so he mounted the bank beside his car, coming level with a newly plowed field which looked over the small valley of some tiny stream, stretching its course seaward, bending several miles to the south where an old town stood, where a church stood, whose bell had summoned him. He found himself sitting down on the old stone wall, and taking in the panorama before him. Before too long, a toot of a large horn indicated that the tow truck had arrived. He was about to praise the driver for his quick response time but the driver spoke first, apologizing for it taking nearly two hours to get there. Something about the big rig being down, and needing two of the smaller ones with the semi. Two hours! He had sat on that wall for two hours?

Later that week he decided to try an experiment. He told his secretary to book his appointments only for the late morning and the late afternoon, and to not ask him about specific times. He instructed her to let those asking for his time to indicate how long they thought they would need. And then he took off his wrist watch and put it into his desk drawer.

On the next Monday he arrived sometime in the morning at the office. He saw the people with appointments in the order they arrived, and gave them his time as they wanted it. He waited for them to signal an end to the meetings. And when the anteroom was empty, he would go for lunch. Returning from lunch the process was resumed, with him immediately speaking to the first person who arrived for an appointment and concluding at the end of whatever time the last person wanted. Sometimes he would arrive in the office to find people waiting for him, and other times he would wait for them. It didn't seem to matter.

And in between the two courses of meetings he would serve himself lunch. He most often took the break first by walking, and walking without purpose other than walking. He would eat when he felt like it, more often than not outside, usually by the river.

His secretary told him that he was amazed, that in all of his years of working in the company there had never been a CEO who saw so many people and still spent so little time in meetings. Time was changing.

He used the freed-up time to open his eyes. From his penthouse office he could see the whole expanse of the city, and usually he took in the full view. But now he began to focus. To look at the elements of the view. To truly see what could be seen.

He was surprised about a week later when a glint of light, bright sun light, poured down a north-south street at nearly sunset. How was this possible? Was he disoriented? Was the light playing a trick on his eyes?

The next day he found his way to that street, at nearly the same time, and suddenly, like a burst of all creation, the sun blinded him, from the north! He squinted, and

The Venice Stories

finally saw the way the glass tower several blocks to the north had become a giant mirror. But wait, its edges were now becoming giant prisms, and on some side streets, viewed for the whole block, the sunset was becoming rainbows. Some people lived in the now red houses, and some in the now orange house, and closer to him simple church stood radiantly violet.

That night he awoke in his bedroom and almost arose with the feeling of dawn's approach until he realized the brightness was the full moon, freed from the overcast clouds, now bathing his world with a lunar whiteness. And just before sunrise in the east, he saw a moonset in the west that delicately tinged the lingering streamers of clouds pastel in a gentleness that took his breath away.

Light was changing.

One morning he noticed, in the darkness of a rainy day, that the trip to the city was longer than it had been the day before in the sun. He began to notice that some of the perfect square blocks of the city were longer than others. When he began to give directions by landmarks rather than distances, people coming to see him said that they had never had such easy trips, they thought it would be longer.

On Sundays he would take walks along the river. Some of the river is out in the open, flowing between two banks of fields, and some of it is under the cover of a canopy of trees, here placid, there rapid. It took him several weeks to realize what was puzzling him about the river until an old farmer commented "Yep, same water here abouts as downstream at my neighbor's." He began to look at streams, rivers, paths, streets, highways, skies, and the universe with a new eye to the plasticity of space in the mind of the beholder.

Space was changing.

After a late night benefit in the city, he suddenly decided to do something very daring. Instead of rushing to his garaged car, he would walk the whole block around. Daring because it was nearly 1am, and the streets looked deserted. Soon his shoes made sole and heel sounds that echoed among shadows and shapes that seemed more fluid than solid. Stopping mid-block, he could hear a dripping tap down some alley, a plaintive meow out of sight, a deep resonant snore from above him, and somewhere in the distance a click-click. At the corner those sounds at first were lost in the traffic noise, but then found their own strength again. Another block , more sounds, and sometimes a deep silence, an expectant silence, which made a non-sound sound.

Sounds were changing.

One Saturday, he went up to the town cemetery. He had no family buried there, but he wondered who was buried there. The names read out like a roster of the town's old line families and the assorted newcomers. Beyond the names, the markers bore the stories of lives, some lived long, others barely lived. Some marked with fraternal and religious symbols, others with military decorations. Some were well maintained and some wanted for a loving hand. When he shared the story of his visit, an old friend thought it all depressing, macabre. And he surprised himself by responding, "Any more depressing or

The Venice Stories

macabre, more hopeful or promising, than the lives they led?" In the question and the silence that was its answer, he realized that for him life was changing.

When he had left Venice that long time ago so recently, he had looked and felt like a shell, a hollow possibility that had once been a full reality. Maybe it was the way that he no longer was time's servant, maybe it was the way that he watched the world of light and dark, of space and shapes, maybe it was the way his ear had become aware of the harmonies of existence surrounding him, maybe it was the way he began to see a reality beyond the edges of life. Maybe it was all of this, and something more which he could not name or describe, which was filling him. That act of being filled felt fulfilling as well, not just of being sated but coming into the being he was beyond this one life.

Spirit was changing.

The following Monday he waited for the "Walk" light to come on at a crowded crosswalk. The light changed and suddenly the intersection was filled with a mass. But what a mass. A hurrying crowd, full of grim faces, sharp tongues, jostled attachés.

Who were these people? Where did they come from? He could not understand it. They were in the midst of the most promising event in the universe, being alive on a day full of time, light, space, sound, life, and spirit . How could they not notice?

Ahead he saw a man who looked vaguely familiar, a man looking full of wisdom and insight, full of awareness and choice. And then he recognized his own reflection in the glass of an advertising kiosk, wearing a knowing smile and a serenity he could not have even imagined.

Suddenly, he felt like Adam, putting his own key into the gates of his own Eden.

Randolph W.B. Becker

THE HAND

Why the hand fascinated her was not immediately obvious to her. She first noticed it gripping the rail of the number 1 boat departing from Venice's Salute dock. She had disembarked to spend some time with the Guggenheim collection while waiting for Harry to finish his own research in the Archivio di Stato. Turning back toward the canal as the boat groaned heavily on its way into the watery commerce of the city, her eyes fastened on a single hand.

It was tanned, strong looking, appearing slightly rough, with a firm grip on the rail amid the crush of the summer's tourists, not that unlike so many other hands on the rail. But it was so unlike those others because something about the hand seemed to speak to her. She quickly scanned the row of faces above the rail for the owner of the hand, but with heads turned, a moving boat, a crowd of possibilities, she could not identify the owner of that hand.

Yet, she knew, in her heart of hearts, she needed to know whose life and being were connected to that hand. Thinking back to what she had observed, she remembered it was a left hand. A left hand without a ring on the ring finger, but with a small gold ring on the pinky and a larger one with a red stone on the middle finger. That larger one had been of delicate proportions that seemed almost out of place with the constructive masculinity of the skin and bones that lay beneath it. The nails had been clean and trim and without decoration. She watched the vaporetto ply off toward San Marco, and with it went feelings of desire and of loss that startled her. A stranger watching her at that moment would have observed her unconsciously shake her head as if to clear it, to return the contents of her thoughts into a more normal pattern. With that she took stock of her surroundings, and started off toward the collection that had summoned her, and the hand (and the feelings it evoked) was relegated to a less active part of her mind. Indeed, when she later met Harry for drinks (where else but at Harry's Bar, a custom they indulged on each Thursday whenever they were in Venice), she made no mention of the incident because she did not remember it.

Their first week of the three passed in the usual fashion ... she and Harry were creatures of habit, the kind of habit that makes delight a product rather than a surprise. Planning and scheduling demanded energy that was expected to be repaid in familiar pleasure. Each trip was parceled out in a two for one mode: two familiar activities for each new venture. *Da Fiore* and *La Caravelle* fed them before they ventured forth to *Iguana*. The Academia and Scuola da Rocco were visited before any of the exhibits of the Biennial. Side trips to Florence and Milan preceded an outing to Verona.

So the days unfolded, bringing the assured first and the possible second, ensuring that whatever happened they would not be disappointed by the trip overall.

Being safe from disappointment was a theme each of

them felt but of which neither of them spoke, even to themselves, much less to each other. She had known the disappointment of her father's less-than-spectacular career that left her feeling unsupported in the competitively material suburb of her teen years. Failure to be accepted by the university of her choice was followed by four years of college wantonness in a vague attempt to ensure popularity which instead left her the abandoned love-interest of more boys than she cared to remember. Harry had been the safe choice, not the first choice, that offered itself in her early work years. He had never disappointed her. He had also never excited her. It was a bargain she accepted so she could feel life had some reliable foundation.

Harry reached for security from a different direction. The intelligent, dutiful first child of a wealthy merchant, he had known little want for material things, but felt he barely knew either of his parents. The life of any party which included him, he provided a seventh generation of graduates from the family's school (though by the time he got there they had opened the doors to women which, in his father's eyes, meant that it was the same school in name only). His place in the family firm was assured, and he took it responsibly the fall after graduation, following his grand tour of Europe. However, even though in the same firm, he saw little of his father, and now living the life of a "man" of the world he saw even less of his mother and home. When, in the following spring, his father's heart, without warning, ceased its support of life, Harry was startled to find that his portion of the estate was

The Venice Stories

symbolic compared to his mother and four sisters. As his father wrote in the will, "Harry has the means, the aptitude, and the schooling to achieve much, while the females of my responsibility have vaguely little to assure them of their own fortunes." Disappointment is too gentle a word for the depth of feeling Harry experienced at that time. Suddenly he was no longer the life of the parties to which he was invited, and the number to which he was invited was far smaller. His life became more loneliness than liveliness. He continued in his position, now part of the corporate machinery more than anointed heir. Two years later he met her at one of those arts events which one attends hoping for companionship but willing to settle for the beauty of the art, so that one will not go home completely empty-handed. She was insightful, intelligent, and not demanding. Harry sensed immediately that should he pursue her, he would be honor bound to never disappoint her. In return, she would hold no surprises for him, not even surprises of passion. It was a bargain he accepted so he could feel that life had some reliable foundation.

On that mutual foundation, their lives had merged. Each as cautious as the other about new ventures, each as certain as the other about known virtues, each as unexpressive as the other of the underlying issues.

A pact sealed in silence.

That silence suddenly parted for her in the second week of the trip, when they were dining at one of the lesser known trattoria with tables on a fondamenta in Dosoduro. The day had been long and enjoyable, including the familiar trips to Murano and the Lido, and now this new place to dine. The food was pleasant, the air warm, and the evening beckoning when the silent dark shape of a gondola drifted past their table, coming from behind her. She was startled out of some small reverie with the gondolier's call of "OY" in time to see, disappearing into the dark night, the hand gripping the side rail of gondola. "Dear," she cried, "did you see who was in that gondola?"

He, seemingly equally caught in his own private thoughts, came back to the present in a disturbed mood, able to only respond, "What?"

"That gondola! Who was in it?"

"How should I know? Why would I be looking at who is in a gondola?"

"Didn't you see who?"

"No, and what difference does it make. Why won't you believe me when I say I don't know? Did you think it was someone you know?" he spit out, almost aggressively.

How could she answer that? No, she did not know that person. But she knew that hand. It had surprised her. And now she had surprised Harry by her sudden outburst. Beating a hasty retreat she suggested, "I thought it looked like the Betts, but now I think of it, they are still in France."

≈≈≈

In sleep as cautious as awake, the two of them had fashioned inner lives that admitted no recognition of dreams. Whatever dreams they each had were hidden so deep that they both honestly stated in conversations about such things that no, they never dream. That night,

The Venice Stories

however, she did dream, and she knew it, and she remembered it. It filled her with excitement and dread.

She dreamt of the hand.

It left its place on a boat rail, and touched her arm. No more than that, but with that touch energy flowed through her whole being. It surprised her, not only the feeling, but that she even felt it.

That was all. A simple touch. Nothing more. And nothing less.

The next day, as she walked the familiar streets of Florence (having come over on the early train) she could feel that touch all over her. Her mind was not on the paintings of the *Uffizio*, but in the presence of *David* she found herself touched by Michelangelo's artistry as never before. She stared at those hands and could almost feel them touching her, like the hand of her dream. That night she dreamed of the hand again. In the darkness of her bed, the hand touched her, and then brought to her side the firmness of a living, breathing David, one of human proportions but divine energy. The hand embraced her, pulling her close. She sobbed a sudden cry of startled pleasure, and almost immediately worried for the disappointment of the end of the dream. But when sleep overcame dream, and she awoke in the morning out of the reach of the hand, she found that she was far beyond any disappointment.

The day began as if the first day of a new life for her. She arose with a sense that she was willing to risk the pain of disappointment to savor, even once more, the thrill she had rediscovered in her dream. But her renewed passion was fueled by obsession. This had all started with the hand. It belonged to the one who came to her dreams. It represented all those lost lovers who, in retrospect, would now desire her company. It represented all those qualities of strength, work, and maleness which could mate with her femininity to do startling things. With such a person, she would never be disappointed and she would always be excited. She must find that hand, and find the person attached to it. She needed to know that touch, that love. Deep streams long suppressed flowed freely, opening her to daring where once only security had been welcomed.

But, of course, she said nothing of this to Harry. He would not understand. It would disrupt his image of her. It would probably disappoint him. He, after all, never showed even the slightest hint of having a thought even vaguely like this. This was hers to have, hers alone.

≈≈≈

Over the next few days, upon their return to Venice, she began to suggest all the more that Harry complete some of the historical research that was his passion; she would pursue some of the sights of more particular interest to her. Harry seemed agreeable (wasn't he always agreeable) to her suggestions, so she found herself free to journey the whole city like the omnipresent tourists. However, whereas most tourists raised their eyes to sights above them, she focused her eyes downward, to hands. On rails, banisters, pew backs, canes, café tables, door knobs, ... she looked to hands.

≈≈≈

She became an expert in hands. She had never noticed

The Venice Stories

how varied they are. Short fingers, long fingers, fat fingers, missing fingers. Smooth skin, pale skin, rough skin, burned skin. Hair, scars, scabs, bandages. Clean, dirty, arthritic, palsied. So many hands, but not the hand.

Days passed, side trips concluded, sights visited, but still no new sighting of the hand.

At least, no new sighting in the waking world, but now nightly the hand would enter her dreams, touching her in ways beyond her wildest dreams, and bidding her all the more to follow. The passion grew, the obsession grew, while the days diminished.

Soon the three weeks were nearly gone, and she felt the pressure of the remaining time. As always, they would have their final dinner on the Giudecca at Cipriani's. Then a late night boat back to San Marco, and a stroll to their hotel; in the morning there would be little time before their flight. So, on that last day, she suggested to Harry that she wanted to spend the afternoon on some things of her own, and would meet him for dinner.

"You are surprising me," Harry responded. "It's not like you."

"O, I guess I have a few surprises left in me"

"Not too many, I trust. Who knows, maybe I have a few surprises left in me too."

"I'll believe that when I see it," she jested.

And off she went, knowing how little Harry would believe it, even if he saw her, as she sought a lover by a hand.

As the day stretched its length toward evening, she was growing more and more disappointed. The slipping light was telling her that she was not likely to find her heart's desire. At last she went to the vaporetto dock to begin the journey toward dinner. At the dock she had to make the decision of whether she would travel there by the regular or the reverse route. Which would reveal more hands? The regular route would be fuller, and hence more hands. And it was into that line she placed herself. A boat came, and the line ahead of her packed itself aboard, but she chose to be first on the next boat rather than last on this one. So, she stood by the looming open gangway with its restraining chain, looking out onto the canal when the reverse boat, having stopped at the other gangway, slowly started to move away. And there, there on the hand rail, was the hand! Her heart nearly stopped.

She quickly looked up from the hand, to see the rest of this spirit of passion and dreams. What she saw took her breath away.

That hand, with all of its strength and power and roughness and energy, was on the arm of a striking, blond-haired, blue-eyed shapely woman.

She had barely taken this in, in excitement rather than disappointment, an excitement which perplexed her but enlivened her, when her eyes took in the rest of the picture: this golden woman standing there, one hand, the hand, on the rail and the other hand ... the other hand ... holding Harry's hand.

THE GIFT

He scarcely took notice of the gentle tapping of the boat's bow against the striped post until a gentle hand touched his shoulder, "Signore, your hotel." He was still miles away, exiting the departure lounge at Dulles with his wife's parting comment ringing in his ears.

"Whatever possessed you to buy me this? O, well, I appreciate the gesture," she had said, bestowing a quick peck on his cheek, "Bon voyage."

The "this" was his farewell gift for her, a warm, soft scarf that he had imagined she could use through the winter for warmth and as a reminder of his love. He had chosen it because he knew she needed it, and it seemed so much "her", and ... he always had a long list of reasons for the gifts he gave her.

Yet, over the years her responses had become painfully familiar. His gifts were met with contemplations of motives ("Why are you giving me *this*?"), incredulity ("What, for *me*?"), intellectual judgment ("What were you thinking?"), or now, the supernatural (the "whatever possessed you ..." burning deeper into his spirit.) Their parting had been more a slipping away to their own, long-developed private worlds than a mournfully felt severing of daily intimacy.

≈≈≈

101

The Venice Stories

Four thousand miles away, a strange hand, some foreign words, unfamiliar stone steps welcomed him. He was suddenly aware, almost too aware, of where he was. This was Venice and he, the arriving traveler, was checking into his hotel for the two nights before his apartment would be available. Most travelers who opt for the expensive water taxi ride from Marco Polo Airport into the city retain vivid memories of their approach to this fabled place, but he suddenly realized that he remembered little of the trip, much less the two airplanes into which he had been crammed. The airplanes were forgettable, of course, as a defense against their inhumane conditions. But that watery entry into history; he told himself that his many previous trips to Venezia had made him a little jaded, a little too worldly. Yet, in his heart he knew it was because her words stung him to the core, stole his heart, and left him half dead.

He would be gone for six months, a full sabbatical semester, and all he brought of his dearest relationship was a rebuke and a peck on the cheek.

But now he was summoned to task, only the fourth interruption of his ruminations since his gift and those words. A plane change, immigration, and transfer of his bags to the water taxi had been but brief interludes in a long period void of activity and full of thought.

A registry to be signed, a passport to be given, a credit card to be swiped and imprinted, a key to carry, a breakfast room to locate, a porter to tip, a room to inspect, a bag to be unpacked, a plan for the evening to be made, a plan for the next day to be started.

A city to be called home.

By Thursday, he was comfortably located in his own apartment, a simple second floor studio near the Ponte delle Gúglie, with a window view out over some terraces toward the Ghetto, and only the faintest hint of the presence of the canals. It had been chosen because of its practical nature: affordable, away from the tourists, quiet, with room for him to write and read, small enough to require little care. It should be easy to settle in, he told himself.

But, the little things confounded his attempts. The Italian towels were too small for his liking, the bed without the upper sheet had a strange feel, the light bulbs were all so dim, the faucets and shower operated peculiarly, even the can opener was shaped so it fit unfamiliarly in his hand. Had all the hotels of his previous trips conspired to present a Venice that was just different enough to be appreciated but not so different as to be disturbing?

His work, however, was familiar: the standard pace of reading, researching, writing. Once he had overcome the perplexity of the telephone plug and connected his laptop, with the aid of access reciprocally provided through the University of Venice, he could function as if he were at home in his study and at home in his studies.

His apartment became his home by becoming a distant image of his home in Maryland. When the random feeling of displacement would strike him, he would use the binding of a familiar volume as a touchstone, its leather a tactical and scented statement of at-homeness. He coped with difference by finding the familiar.

The Venice Stories

But, the Venetian light, the ever-present bouquet of sea and antiquity, the phantom fog does not yield its difference easily. One can no more neatly map out one's senses and emotions there than one can reduce the maze of sea and land to a logical set of highways and byways. He felt this so intensely that at first he allowed himself passage beyond his apartment only to a nearby bar and to the most familiar tourist sites. He experienced the city more as a postcard review than as his life.

All that changed in his second month, when the returning sun of spring finally found a portion of his window open to its rays, and a corner of his familiar room entertained this welcomed stranger many mornings. But when, by late morning, its brilliance moved on to those with a more westerly prospect, he felt himself called to follow its beams. He resisted the urge for several days, but the primordial tug on his soul was too insistent, and like a bear greeting spring, he emerged from his room, from his house, from his work, from his established pattern, to walk beside the Cannaregio Canal and soak in the sun, and the people, and the boats, and something more.

≈ ≈ ≈

He could feel it flooding into his spirit, and he remembered it from long ago in his life. It was a spirit of invitation to explore, once alive in the wild woods of Wisconsin, then in the uncharted realms of intense late-night debate with teenaged friends, then in university offerings beyond his wildest dreams, and even in his pursuit of the then o-so-dangerous one with whom he now shared married life.

So, he ventured forth, first into the immediate neighborhood and its labyrinth of *Calli* and *Fondamenta*. Then, to the more distant parts of the city. He began to rub shoulders on the *Motoscafo* with both tourists and Venezianos, and followed their talk and their walk to new bars and restaurants he had never before glimpsed. It was almost like he had to substitute a pattern that was all-new in order to be able to move out of his pattern of familiar sameness.

When, towards midnight he would return home (for now he considered the apartment his home), he would find himself filled with delicacies of life, tidbits of humanity. On the next morning, over the cappucino, he would find his work not only flowed more easily, it was richer, deeper, more satisfying. The very act of reaching out (out from the apartment, out from the familiar) allowed him to also reach in (into life, into himself, into ... something he could not name).

By the end of the third month, as the tourist hordes began their great shoulder-season descent on the city, he found himself day after day watching the activity of the canals, lagoons, and city from that sharp point of land at the Customs House in Dorsoduro, the place where land meets water, sky meets earth, east meets west, physical meets spiritual. On the one side the last shafts of day would filter through the edges of buildings, while on the other side night had already beckoned the soft glow of the pink lights. Here was his place, his moment at the turning of eternity, his point between past and future. Each night he approached that spot with anticipation and some dread,

The Venice Stories

sensing a call to be there and apprehensive about what might be asked of him.

≈≈≈

A series of rainy days had kept him from his usual ritual. The *aqua alta*, too late into the season by the account of many, made his "spot" unaccessible as well. When, at last, the air and the land were both dry enough to allow his presence, he eagerly (surprising even himself in his eagerness) found his way from the *Salute* stop, along the ancient stone walkways to that point of arrival and departure.

Once more the sea and the sky greeted him, each tinged a bluish-pink in mirrored imitation of each other. "Ah," he thought, but no words came. "Ah."

"Signore," the voice said in a surprisingly unstartling way.

"Mi fa accendere, per piacere?" the stranger asked. An expectant cigarette dangled in his one hand, the other hand making a pleading gesture, pointing toward it.

"No, sorry," was all he could muster.

"Ah, Englisha, yes?" the stranger responded.

"No, American."

"From Dallas?" returned the too familiar question; TV had raised many expectations in the minds of Europeans about the life styles of most Americans.

"No, Maryland," he had answered, suddenly aware of two conflicting thoughts competing for his brain's attention. The first had quickly transposed Dallas into Dulles, and replayed the now usually forgotten farewell scene. The second was that he had already told this stranger too much, that he should be more guarded.

"Okay, near Washington," the stranger continued as if a conversation of some familiarity had already been established. "Do you work for the government?"

In his familiar reflex to this perennial question posed to anyone who lived near DC, he blurted out, "No, I teach at the University - Medieval Studies. I'm here on a sabbatical." already worrying all the more about giving too much information as he heard himself speak the words.

"Ah,", the stranger said, "A colleague. I am instructor in Medieval and Renaissance Art. I am, this term, yes, you say term, visiting speaker here at University."

With that he moved his cigarette from his hand to his mouth, and offered his hand in greeting. "Paolo"

"John," he replied, placing his hand, and his trust, in the grip of this stranger.

With that the pact was signed what would unfold over the next months. The first evening it was a short exchange of words about Venice, about living away from family, about work; some small talk that could have absorbed the moments of a cocktail party while another round of drinks was being sought. Before long, each had wished the other *"Buona sera"* and gone their separate ways, he along the Grand Canal, and Paolo toward the Záttere.

As he walked toward home, he found himself more moved by the encounter than he would have expected previously. Something was happening. Was it happening to him? In him? With him?

≈≈≈

He did not find the answer for three days, as the rains

returned with a vengeance, this time sparing the city the high water with more favorable winds. The clearing skies of the afternoon of the third day were a welcomed relief; he had holed himself up in the apartment and worked feverishly through the patter of the rain on the marble terrace floor above his study area. It was nearly sunset when he reached the point, and the absolute point was already occupied with someone standing astride the two sides, like some figurehead on the ship of Venetian state. As he approached, he caught the whiff of smoke and a vaguely familiar scent.

"Paolo?" he called, surprising himself at his eagerness to connect.

"John," the figure replied, and he was greeted with the open arms of an embrace, of an intimacy between men that is as foreign in America as it is common in Italy.

"Tonight we celebrate the good weather, yes? We find some drink first, and then some food?"

What could one say to this openness, the invitation, this inclusion, this connection, but "yes."

That evening of wine, then conversation, then food, then more conversation, then espresso and more conversation, was the beginning of a pattern that developed quickly and firmly in the days to follow.

No plans were ever made for the next evening, or Saturday next week, or for any specific time. But when the two of them would meet, sometimes at that point of connection, and other times at very different places about the city, the one who had been the "guest" the last time (although each always paid his own way) became the "host", proposing another evening of sustenance of body, mind, and spirit. The host always selected the venue, the guest always the initial topic of discussion.

Now his days were filled more than ever before with feelings of completion and fulfillment. His research blossomed, his writing flowed, and his understanding deepened. Once or twice, in a moment of quiet reflection, he would marvel how his relationship with Paolo was so different from his other relationships. Unlike what he felt in all of his amorous relationships (successful or otherwise), there was no sexual tension here. Nor was there dependency, or a sense of servitude, or a sense of responsibility. The roles were simple, respectful, and equal. He could say whatever he liked ("so what if Paolo gets offended?"). He could be as open or closed as he wished, and with that freedom he found himself more open than he ever imagined he would be with any other person. He felt himself being himself in relationship for the first time. Yes, the first time. This was so different from being himself with parents, brothers and sisters, relatives, teachers, lovers, partner, co-workers, bosses, neighbors. With each of them he was that part of himself that related to them; most of him was still buried somewhere inside. He wanted it that way (for safety? for ease? for ...?) and it always seemed that they wanted it that way too. With Paolo it was different. He did not spend time or energy pining or planning, wondering or worrying.

There was the night that he and Paolo argued over euthanasia. From an agreement on the sacredness and beauty of life they diverge to two, resolutely opposing

The Venice Stories

points of view. He found himself trying to out-shout Paolo, waving his fist in rage at misinterpreted comments, and finally calling Paolo "an ignorant, regressive, pseudo-intellectual fascist worthy of Mussolini."

That was the night that Paolo later put his arm around his shoulder as they walked and said quietly, "We make good argument, yes? You know how we do that? We be ourselves."

≈≈≈

"We be ourselves," he had agreed, and realized how often that had been true. Rather than trying to connect to Paolo's habit, he had refused the offered cigarettes. Paolo would not select wines to match the dinner as he would have, but selected wines on whim it seemed. He had refuted a key point in Paolo's research on Titian. Paolo uncovered the plagiarism of one of his main sources. What he did or did not do or say was not conditioned on how Paolo would react to it. It seemed the same for Paolo. "We be ourselves," became their catch-phrase of appreciation.

As the fifth month closed, and the sixth was already progressing, he realized that a time of departure was coming. Paolo would go back south to Roma, and he would return to Maryland. The relationship, as it had been, was coming to an end. Yes, there could be emails, and promised future visits, but it would not be the same. Here, in this magical city, freed of so many constraints of the rest of life, family, and habitual work, something unique had grown. How could it be honored, celebrated, and commemorated?

With about three weeks to go, he began to search for a

gift to give to Paolo. Paolo was scheduled to leave after he was; Paolo's family was coming to Venice for some days, and then they all were off for holiday in the Dolomites.

His daily routine shifted, with work scheduled only in the mornings (he was now only editing the material so thoroughly documented and expressed), evenings left for Paolo or such other activities of Venice as caught his eye, and afternoons seeking his gift for Paolo.

Remembered conversations, observed habits, patterns of dress, books mentioned, music liked (and hated) – he considered them all. What would Paolo like? What did Paolo need?

Venice is nothing if not a place to shop for gifts. Hundreds upon hundreds of shops offer everything from trinkets to antiques to glass to jewelry to scent to books to the treasures of all the world. However, as promising as each shop might appear on entry, all became depressingly empty of the right gift upon closer inspection.

One day, on one of the back alleys in Sao Polo, in a store offering the classic Venetian masks of *Carnivale*, a curious old shopkeeper, bent with age and service, asked him a simple question, "Is this for yourself or for someone else?"

He suddenly found he could not speak. Not in English, or Italian. His heart and mind and spirit were at once pierced to their core and opened to the light.

"We be ourselves."

The gift he needed to give to Paolo was not about Paolo, but about himself. That is what he had always given in the relationship, himself. Paolo took care of himself.

The Venice Stories

The search of obligation turned into a search of exultation and celebration of self. Upon entering a shop, he would look to see what spoke to his soul, to his eye, to his being. Where did he see himself reflected? What object embodied part of his spirit?

Not long into the search he found himself returning again and again to a small glass shop off Piazza San Marco, to look at a unique glass box in the display case toward the rear. It was irregularly shaped with an equally irregularly shaped lid, all fashioned out of some of the deepest shades of Murano glass he had seen. From above it look like a dark iris exploding. From the side, depending one where you looked, like a waterfall, a butterfly, a smiling Madonna, a sunset over water. Inside one thought immediately of a geode made of rainbows baked to golden, iridescent hues. He could imagine the box on his own work table, holding small bits of this and that that were treasures only to him. He could see himself getting lost in its contemplation when work became too much.

Finally he asked to see the box outside the case. The clerk, offering the usual solicitudes about quality, Murano, taste, and price, set it on a velvet cloth on the counter. It radiated some kind of energy. It drew him into itself like a spiritual magnet. He asked to touch it, and with reluctance was given permission. He could barely bring himself to actually touch it, the sense of energy was so strong, but once he lifted it he felt as if he held his own throbbing heart in his hands.

≈≈≈

The formalities seemed endless. A price to be agreed

upon. Cash or credit card? Receipts to be made. Shipped or taken? Is this a gift? Wrapped, but of course. Endless.

All he wanted to do was take the box with him and give it to Paolo.

The gift wrapping seemed to have a special effect on the box, for as he carried it carefully on his arm, it now felt like its energy was sealed for another to experience. He could carry it without it overcoming him. Now its intense energy gave back to him rather than demanded from him. He walked toward the Rialto and on toward home with a sense of liveliness he had never felt before.

He had thought about the moment of giving throughout the search. He wanted to give his gift to Paolo at their last occasion together before Paolo's family arrived and he was too absorbed in his own departure. So, on the night before Paolo would become a family man again and he would depart, he strolled the streets all afternoon, carrying his gift with him. Toward sunset he approached the point of beginnings and ending, of sunrise and sunset, sure he would find Paolo there. But, the point was his alone, until long after twilight had become evening. This resolved matters for him. He made his way toward the Zattere, and Paolo's apartment. Neither had ever gone to the other's home, although both knew where the other lived; it was an unspoken respect for that space of one's needed privacy. At the door, he hesitated, and then knocked.

No answer.

A second knock, and this time the door below opened.

The Venice Stories

"Signore," a voice called.
"Si"
"Signore John?"
"Si!"
"Ho una lettera per lei, il signore."
"Grazie"
A letter, with his name on it.
Inside a brief note:
"John - I try to call you all afternoon. My car, my family, broken on the Autostrada. Only car hurt. I must go immediately. I give you my friendship. Paolo"

The old lady then handed him a book, in Italian, with Paolo's name on the title page. Below was his expansive writing: "We be ourselves. That time in Venezia. Paolo"

"Grazie" he repeated.

He arrived home realizing, through his periodic tears (What were those about? Who were they for?) that he was feeling more appreciation than loss, for a gift had been given – the time with Paolo. It did not take the presentation of his gift to validate what each had given the other. He sighed, and watched the crescent moon slip slowly beyond the lagoon before turning down his calle and into his house.

In the morning he had no time to pack and mail the package to Paolo. His own packing, neglected in the emotions of the last evening, was now hastily done, until at last he came to the precious gift. Placing it in the center of his softest clothing in his carry-on bag, he gently covered it with the soft sweater he had worn on arrival and closed the case.

His departure was not unlike his arrival. He scarcely noticed the details of passage, from apartment to water taxi to airport, from airplane to airplane. But, this time he was overcome by emotions that made him feel full rather than empty.

Somewhere about 100 miles from touchdown at Dulles, as the flight attendants were making the cabin ready for arrival, he felt summoned. Later he could not say that it was in the form of words or even images: he simply knew what he had to do.

Taking his carry-on from the overhead bin, he opened it carefully and took out the still-wrapped gift. He returned the bag to the bin, but kept the gift in his lap, caressing it gently with his hands as the plane landed and taxied to its gate. Through immigration and customs, the gift was his guarded companion. Even when he surrendered his bags to a porter to take to the curb, he kept the gift with him.

Emerging from the cocoon of transit into the arrival area, he could see his wife among the many people searching for a familiar face. As he approached her, he held out the gift, almost like a mother presents a newborn to be held by another. His wife received the package with a startled, almost apprehensive look. Removing the wrapping, she revealed the packing box and then the contents, and stood for a moment speechless.

"Whatever possessed you to buy me this?" she asked, and then added quickly, "It is so, so you. And it is so, so beautiful. O, John, this is the most wonderful gift you have ever given me." And with that she embraced him, fiercely. Her arms felt more accepting and comforting than he had

The Venice Stories

ever known before. Hand in hand, they walked out of the terminal, his gift carried by both of them.

THE FIGHT

It began in the center of Piazza San Marco.

Well, actually it probably began many years ago, on the first day they met.

But it erupted in the center of Piazza San Marco.

Right in the middle of Carnevale, in the midst of that great throng of masked revelers, they went at it.

He was hungry, thirsty, and tired, and a bathroom would have been welcomed. He wanted, more than anything else at that moment, to get to a restaurant, any restaurant, and have his needs met. So, he said simply, "Look, let's just get out of this mob, go someplace and eat."

And she replied, just as simply, "Sure, let's start looking at places to see where we might like to eat tonight."

With that, he turned on her and growled through his mask, "I didn't say I want to look at restaurants, I said I want to go to one!"

"Don't get huffy with me. I just don't want to waste an evening in this town on some mediocre food."

"Sure, just like always. How about this place? No, it doesn't look right. How about this place? No, it doesn't smell right. This place? No, the menus look old. This place? Well, maybe, but let's keep looking. Maybe that first place was better. Always have to look. Treat even the

The Venice Stories

simplest life task like a shopping trip!" By now he was yelling at her.

And she yelled right back.

"Look, everyday at home I have to make choices about what will be the best foods to serve, and how best to serve them, so when you get home you get what you consider a good meal. For me, a vacation is a time to not have to do the work, but have the pleasure of choosing where I will eat, to get what I want as I want it for my dinner." The last part of the sentence was spit out at a very, slow, paced cadence, each word having it own place in the echoes of the Piazza.

("God," he thought, "what a shrew.")

But what he said was, in equally measured terms, "I did not know that our dinner was a matter of only your choice."

"About the only thing I do get to choose!"

"Well, then, why don't you just go and choose all you want. I am going to eat."

And he turned from her and strode off, away from her, lost almost immediately in the vast crowd.

He walked away so fast he did not hear her parting comment, "Go ahead, find some poor excuse of tourist food. Without **me** you wouldn't know fettuccine from linguine." And she then turned to face in the other direction.

≈≈≈

His immediate path was out of the Piazza, toward the Accademia Bridge, moving quickly into the tight warren that is the walkways of Venice.

His longer path was out of a childhood of recognized competence and brilliance into the academic and social challenges of college. Even stacked up against the best of the best, he was the one who was tapped over and over again for leadership positions. His advice was sought by his peers because he was known for his insight, his integrity, his creativity, and his intellect. When he spoke, people did not just listen. They acted, and acted as he suggested.

Plays were directed, newspapers edited, student rallies organized, university senate meetings presided over, and academic accolades accepted.

If anyone were competent, assured, respected, he was it.

(Well, in the eyes of everyone else, but himself, if the truth be told. He always expected that sooner or later, probably sooner, someone would see through the facade to the needy, unsure, unworthy person that was the real him.)

He met her in the middle of his doctoral program, post-qualifying-exams, pre-thesis. What appealed to him about her was that she did not put him on the pedestal from which he knew he would eventually fall. With her, it felt like the inevitable fall would be shorter.

He would talk, and she would not wait on his every word. She would not object to what he was saying, but instead would imply her own better understanding.

He would act, and she would not follow his lead. She would decisively choose another path as if he were some wandering idiot.

The Venice Stories

He would focus his attentions on her, and she would not seem to notice. She would repel the advances as if the attention was thoroughly unwanted.

And so, he talked, acted, focused all the more, always with her in mind.

It was a great challenge.

If he could win over this perverse beauty, he might, after all, have some measure of worth as a human being.

In the fullness of time and his unending attention to her, she finally began to evidence some response that was more positive than negative.

She relented to his offer of a date. He was solicitous of her thoughts of what to do and where to go. Of course, he made suggestions, but let her make the final decision.

It always felt, in the beginning, that she was honoring his many suggestions like they were all valuable gems, and her role was to sift through them to find the diamond among the rubies and emeralds. He liked that. It made him feel valued. His relationship with her felt like all of his other relationships with the big exception that she did not seem to have a clue as to the inner jelly of his insecurities. She genuinely seemed to like all of him, and value what he was and did: by not valuing it too highly or liking him too much.

≈≈≈

She had liked all of him, and did value what he was and did.

Of course she would, given how her life had unfolded.

As he disappeared from her sight in the Piazza, she did what she always did. She just stood there, not wanting to even look at his disappearance. She just stood, and thought of all the things that were wrong with what was happening, and especially all that was wrong with him, no actually with her.

Of course, it must be wrong with her. That is what she had been taught. The last child, and the only girl in a very patriarchal family, she was not expected to excel at anything other than amiability. Her A's were never received as well as the RBI stats of her brothers. Her piano recital was neglected because one or another brother had a basketball game.

It did not take her long to figure out that she did not matter for much in the scheme of things. Her opinion was not sought.

So, she developed her own strategy for not only survival but standing in her family. She became the family critic.

In the midst of any of the planning for what the family would do, always among the "men of the family" while her mother was busy in the kitchen, she would look for and announce any problem with the proposed plan.

"That would be fine," she would say, "if you were doing it on Saturday, but they are closed on Sundays."

After disastrously ignoring her warnings on a few occasions, the family came to listen to her, never as the first resort, but only as the last resort. Her power and standing in the family grew as she honed this skill. At first she never spoke before she was sure she had information enough to be decisive. Over time she engaged in active participation in the process, asking for those bits of

The Venice Stories

information she would need. In her own mind she called it "shopping for problems."

One day, when she was about 8, her next older brother beat her up. Well, not really that bad, but enough of a threat to scare her. As he finished half-heartedly pounding on her arms, he spat out, "All you are is a problem maker. Just stop it!"

Not wanting to live out her life with sore arms, she realized she needed to change her approach. So, she became the judge of success rather than failure. Turning her former method around, she began to indicate which of the family proposals had the greatest chance for working. Now she thought of herself as "shopping for success."

This mode served her well in school, where she was never asked into any leadership positions but was always consulted by the power brokers of the elementary school world.

"What do you think of this idea for the school trip?" was a question from students and teachers alike.

By middle school, she had her skills perfected. She never advocated anything, she merely analyzed. After all, in the grand scheme of things she knew that she was not a leader, not a mover and shaker, not someone of great worth. The best she could do was comment from the sidelines while the real players, the important people, carried the ball.

College was a big challenge to her. The skill she had crafted for herself served her well in the academic work, where the ability to focus on the worth of an argument, idea, or book was highly rewarded. However, it was not a skill she held alone. Others, she discovered, had found their own way to the same point of view.

One of her early roommates said she thought of it as "trolling for truth," and she had all she could do not to immediately admit to "shopping for success." But, she knew that her power lay in her own secretive use of her insights. To disclose was to disarm.

Then, in her senior year, she met this grad student who seemed to her like a perfect candidate for her efforts. He had been the student body president as an undergrad, and in him she saw all the power, influence, standing she could ever want. With him around, no brother would pound on her ever again.

Even in graduate work, he was a stunning success. He had passed his candidacy exams in record time for his department. When he took her to student and faculty gatherings (he got to go to both because he was a teaching fellow), she stood by him in awe, as much in awe of the fact that she was standing by him as by him.

And she loved the way that he loved the way that she operated.

He was so solicitous of her opinions.

She especially remembered that first date. She had been teasingly trying to get his attentions for a long time, using her time-honored techniques. Show him how competent she could be, but let him make the moves. Not be seen as the "problem maker".

At last she decided enough hints of offers had passed, and she said yes to a date. To her surprise, he did not immediately tell her what they would be doing, like some

The Venice Stories

kind of father figure. He offered a long list of possibilities and asked her which she thought was best. This was the man for her!

≈≈≈

Not long after he had left the Piazza and entered the tangled web that are the walkways, bridges, and canals of Venice, the gentle day turned to night, and with it came the *nebbia*, that thick cloud of fog. It began to seep upward from the canals, around corners of the *Campi*, layering itself on the ancient stones. In a matter of minutes, vistas went from clarity to cloudiness to obscurity. One could not look down even the shortest of the *calli* and see the other end. He felt lost.

But he often felt lost.

He had all the credentials for success – personality, education, and connections – and the realities of success – position, money, and security – yet the prevailing feeling he had lately was of being lost.

He would find himself chairing a meeting and even while steering the direction of the meeting he would be asking himself why anyone should listen to him. He was making it up as he went along, and they were buying it. What if someone were to finally step back and take a look at it all. He would be found out! Unmasked!

And worst of all, the very person who should have been his greatest supporter was the one who kept lifting the mask and telling him to come out of there. His wife no longer treated anything he did or said as if it were a treasure needing evaluation. Now it felt to him like she treated it all like refuse to be sorted into that which needed to be buried and that which could be recycled to better ends. Where once she had been quick to respond to him with ideas on how to build on his ideas to even greater heights, now she wanted to endlessly, yes endlessly, go over the details of what he thought, what he said, what they said, what happened. It was just like tonight. He wanted to eat; she wanted to talk about the process of choosing where to eat. Where once he would have proposed a list of specific restaurants from which she would pick one (and he had to admit she had the uncanny ability to always pick the best one), now he dared only propose the idea of eating, and even that had become open to challenge. What would be next, he wondered. Would he become a post-Cartesian who, when he posed the classic *Cogito ergo sum*, would be greeted with her response, "I need to consider that and other alternatives and get back to you. Until then, don't count on being."

He felt like his role had become a wall, against which she would bounce her ideas like practice tennis balls.

≈≈≈

He suddenly realized that in his rage of thought, he had walked through the swelling fog into an area of the city unknown to him. Had he crossed the Accademia Bridge? Had he turned left or right? Passed the remains of *Le Fenice*?

He had to admit it. Usually he would joke that "I may not know where I am, but I am not lost." This time he was lost.

And he was surprisingly alone.

In the quiet of the fog he could not hear any other

The Venice Stories

footsteps. No lights came from shop windows or upper residential windows.

He was lost and alone.

And he realized that he had lost his mask.

≈≈≈

She stood where she was, with all of the action of *Carnevale* swirling around her, lost in her own thoughts until she realized that her legs were suddenly feeling cold. Around her ankles, despite all the movement of bodies around her, the fog was beginning to engulf San Marco. The street lights, which have been distinct a few moments before at twilight's first gleam, were now more auras than lights, casting specters more than shadows.

She realized that she could not stay where she was. She could not stand there forever, although part of her longed to have someplace she could just stand and be herself for as long as she wanted, maybe forever.

She needed to make her way to the hotel. Yes, that was the best choice. The hotel. But which way. She scanned the Piazza for some clue. But the fog was beginning to obscure her visual access to the information she needed. Without knowing what she needed, how was she to decide?

She felt abandoned.

Utterly abandoned.

And she had been feeling that for a long time now.

She had been abandoned by her family, who saw her marriage as the end of their responsibility for her, and the beginning of her responsibility for them. It was now her turn, as the female head of the next generation, to host all of the family events. She was expected to be hospitable to those people, and their now expanding broods, who once had no use for her, saw no future for her, who beat her arm sore. So, she had turned inhospitable to them, suggesting the best restaurants for social gatherings rather than their home, where everyone, including herself, could have a good time. And without so much as a good argument about it, the family parties moved elsewhere, and she was abandoned by them.

In a world of couples, she had known a role, being one of the twos who would gather during her husband's early career. People looked to her for her sage advice about apartment locations, furniture sources, restaurants, and even career choices. He had often said how proud he was of her, but she knew it could never match the pride she felt in watching him, in social, work, and domestic situations. She knew that the best choice of all the best choices she had ever made was him. He was strength itself. He was knowledge and courage and sociability. Her wisdom of discernment was just an adornment to his powerful presence.

With him she felt that despite all the feelings of abandonment she experienced, she would never be truly alone.

But that feeling was continually being tested. When couples became threes and the talk turned from bistros to babies, from fettuccine to formulas, from linens to layettes, she was left behind, and felt abandoned by the people she had called her friends.

As he had climbed the corporate ladder, she found he brought less and less of the office home with him. Maybe he thought he was doing her a favor, but she had always enjoyed the talk about his work. She had enjoyed knowing what he was thinking about and doing, and adding whatever she could to help him in the decisions he faced. He was still there at dinner, now even more often than when he had been working his way up, but it still felt like a major part of him had abandoned her. He brought nothing home which could engage her side of their partnership.

In her own work, her progress as a corporate troubleshooter had been spectacular, almost vertical. He had joked early on, "So, which position is it this quarter?" A1 had become B1, and then B3, and then C1 and quickly C4, until she had passed beyond the alphabetic levels into levels where the titles were made for the people, not the people chosen for the positions. And then suddenly, about two years ago, she went through an entire year without a change. At first it felt good, to have one's feet planted firmly in one place. But when the same issue came to her attention for decision on a third occasion in ten months, she realized that her elevator had been turned into a waiting room. Slowly the news would filter into her space: this one had moved to the tenth floor, that one had been sent to the London office, and another one was now up in the penthouse. When one of the people she had helped the most in the beginning with suggestions of best choices was sent to the great green glass tower of headquarters, she knew what the feeling was that nagged at her.

She felt abandoned.

And lately, even on the smallest and most intimate level, she felt that he was moving away from her. The easy, almost playful way that they had made life meaningful and enjoyable together was missing more and more. He seemed to resent the role he and she had both cast her into. He would not play their shared interpersonal game anymore.

And now this.

And there, in the middle of the greatest square of the world, in the middle of one of the largest throngs to ever fill that square, in the embrace of the almost primal fog, with a feeling of deep abandonment, she knew how utterly alone she felt, and how utterly lost she felt.

Her smiling, clown-like face paint slowly smeared to a sagging frown as tears trailed down her face.

≈≈≈

He was almost desperate.

No, he was desperate.

He was lost.

He was alone.

And he did not have the one resource with him he most needed.

At each intersection, with the outcomes of the many destinations obscured by the fog, he found himself saying aloud, "Which one do you think is the best one, dear?" wishing frantically that he would hear her reassuring voice beside him saying "This one." Then he could her lead back to familiarity, knowing she always chose correctly. If only she were there, he would not have to be confronting his own ineptitude, his own failure, his own aloneness, his amazing uncertainty at each and every corner. Had she not, over all the years, been the one who had kept him

The Venice Stories

from the great abyss of his own knowing, all the while seeming to know but not care? Wouldn't she be the only one who, in this situation, would focus more on her solution than on his failure to know? Wouldn't she point anywhere he needed to go?

≈≈≈

She was almost despondent.

No, she was despondent.

She was abandoned.

She was alone.

And she did not have the one resource with her she most needed.

In her mind, dozens of scenarios played out, each based on one of the exits from the Piazza. As she came to a conclusion about which would be the best one to take, she found herself saying aloud, "OK, dear, we should go that way!" wishing almost frantically that he would then take her arm and guide her through the crowd and the fog through the exit and to some place of safety and connection and understanding. If only he were here, she would not have to be confronting her own feelings of unworthiness, her own doubts, her own aloneness, and her lack of feeling of empowerment not in what should happen next, but what would actually happen next. Had he not been the one over all of these years who had put action behind her choices, helping her to feel like a whole person and not just some empty shell of choices? Wouldn't he be the only one who, in this situation, would focus more on implementing her solution than on his failure to have his own? Wouldn't he lead her anywhere she chose to go?

≈≈≈

When the fog comes to Venice, everything changes. Monuments become misty mysteries. Piazza and Campi become empty deserts. Bold hearts become timid and timid hearts become bold. Shutters are closed and many move inside. Others walk through the quiet outside. The waterbuses abandon all measure of schedules and routes, and find their way as best that radar and hope can propel them. At some stops two boats come in a direction one immediately after another, and then half an hour of wait ensues before the next.

Following the backs of strangers, she made her way out of San Marco, and surprised herself by leaving not under one of the arcades but rather by the broad expanse leading past the Doge's Palace. Then she remembered that she had turned away when he had left. She had been standing disoriented all that time, and so that among the many choices under the arcade she might have made, none could have been the best, all would have been bad. She had even abandoned herself. So, she just followed, letting others decide, not feeling the need to make the choices. Their decision, or just herd instinct, brought them to the Vaporetto station at San Zaccaria, and there, after some time had passed, she boarded the number 1 boat toward Piazzale Roma, toward their hotel. She drifted to her right, and stood along the starboard rail, almost crushed into that position by the crowd.

After twisting and turning this way and that, he suddenly realized that he was seeing the same darkened storefronts again and again. He was more desperate than

The Venice Stories

ever. And then he saw him, a sole walker in the fog like himself. Abandoning all of his instincts to decisiveness and control, he chose to follow that man, who did not seem to hesitate at any corner, but walked with the confidence of someone who knew where he was going. In this manner he followed for what seemed an eternity in that darkened shroud, long enough to give him some rest from his desperation, long enough for him to not feel so lost, not so alone. Long enough for him to think, and not just panic. And he suddenly realized that he was not simply following this man, he was choosing to follow him. He was putting himself in charge by letting someone else be in charge. He could fail, and it would be all right. He didn't always have to have the best answer, only know how to listen for the best answer when it was given. And the man did not fail him. He led them both to the expanse in front of the Accademia, with the glowing presence of the vaporetto dock nearby. After a long wait, a crowded boat arrived, and he wedged himself aboard, tucked neatly against the port rail.

Stops loomed up out of the fog, and then disappeared back into the fog behind the boat. At last the boat reached San Marcuola. She was one of the first off, heading up the ramp and around the back of the church. He was one of the last off, following the crowd disembarking, hoping against hope that the crowd would stay together as a collective guide for him. But, at the rear of the church, about half peeled off to the right, not his direction. Then, more went to the next right, and the rest to the third right, and he suddenly found himself facing the choice of two narrow passages straight ahead, a small campo to his left, and the wider way to the right. His desperation was returning. Feeling himself quite, no, utterly alone, he said to himself and the fog, "Now, what would be the best way?"

And from somewhere straight ahead a voice he knew like the beating of his own heart answered back, through the fog and what sounded like tears, "There is no best way. But if you come here, we can find our way together, wherever that may lead." And his heart re-chose to follow the only voice that he knew could take him where he needed to go.

THE CITY

THE CANALS

Most of the cities of the world pulse with the rhythms of human creation. At the rise of the sun, people flow into and out of the cities. Horses and donkeys bear their burdens. Bicycles, cars, trams, boats, and trains all hum to their tasks of transportation. Toward the setting of the sun, the flow is reversed: most of those who went out, come in; most of those who came in, go out. At the core of almost all the cities of the world, from the ancient creations of Mayans, Egyptians, Chinese, and so many other cultures to the most modern designs of planned urbanism, have been the roads by which this pulse of the city is facilitated.

But there are a few cities where the pulse is not human, where something else flows more centrally through the city, giving that city its own unique vitality.

Venice is one of those cities, where water is more central to the life flow than are the humans who inhabit it. Indeed, the whole enterprise of being human in Venice depends on this aqueous medium of existence.

Twice daily the sea's own pulse, powered by the moon's attraction, washes in, and twice daily that same

The Venice Stories

pulse washes out. Sometimes, by the conspiracy of wind, lunar phase, and inland rains, that pulse becomes so strong that it dictates an end to normal city life for an hour or two. Boats stop. Walkways flood. Lunches or dinners are lingered over, waiting for the pulse to abate. Shopping trips are delayed. Tardy employees need to offer no excuses. Life goes on, but on the terms of the canals.

It was along one of those canals that he found himself one evening. Not a special evening in his life, or at least not when it began. It was, however, a special evening in the life of the canals, for the pulse was coming on strong, inching the tide upward along canal walls until its would spill across the walkways.

He had been eating a very late lunch in a small osteria in a sestier foreign to him. The night was windy and balmy. A storm was brewing somewhere out in the Adriatic, but its presence was only the east wind and some high thin clouds. His path from the osteria was easy ... along this canal to the motoscafo stop, and then a pleasant ride back. But, already his way was not as easy as when he had arrived, for now he had to navigate around several places where the canal was creeping over its banks. At the waterbus stop, the entry ramp canted abruptly upward. He waited, and waited, for the scheduled boats, but none came. So, now facing an uncertain course back, he carefully made his way down the ramp and back towards where he had dined. But, almost immediately he saw that his way was blocked by waves of water where once there had been very dry stones. Looking to his left, he saw a dry path, and moved hopefully in that direction. But, this was unknown territory.

He could only guess which calle to take, which bridge to cross. At several junctions his choices were limited by liquid barriers. After what seemed like an eternity, he found himself in a narrow passageway that promised a long, through path toward familiar ground. But, that promise was dashed as it ended in a too full canal across which spanned no bridge and whose fondamente was already flooded. Dead end!

Turning back to retrace his steps to his last point of choice, he caught a strange glint toward the other end of the passage. Approaching the glint, he saw it for what it was, the front ripple of the rising water.

Stopping in his tracks, he looked from the unavailable escape in the way he had come and the impossibility of his moving in the way that he was going. And suddenly, in that narrow passageway, with no desirable route to his own sense of safety, his emotions felt scarily familiar. Didn't he feel this way most of the time ... in his less-than-spectacular studies, in his uninspiring job, in his loveless marriage, in his whole narrow passageway of life between a past he could not revisit and any future he could obtain. In school his nickname had been simply, "No," based on his most often used work. A loner, when asked to join in some project or game, he would simply say "no." At work they called him "The pessimist," as he so often worked alone, finding the worst-case scenarios for every proposal. Invitations to office parties and outings were always declined ... "it'll probably rain that day, anyway." His wife, once drawn to a person who seemed to see life realistically

The Venice Stories

and depend on no one, now often avoided the man she called "Gloomy Gus" to her friends. Long ago she knew he would rather do it himself ... find their destination, revamp the flower beds, fix the TV remote ... than have to share his expectation of failure with someone else.

And here he was again, as always, alone, needing to rely on his own wits, seeing no good prospect in any direction, facing the eternal scream that sat at the edge of his every moment. He swallowed hard, as if a physical action could keep that emotional outburst from rising to voice.

Just then a door behind him opened. "Signore," a voice was saying, "Prego!" A gesturing hand indicated entry to the inside, to a long stairway that rose to the house above. He felt the well-practiced "no" forming in his throat, but this man was still speaking, rambling on in Italian. He could catch only a few words, "acqua," "casa," "si?" He tried to signal by gestures what he could not say, but now this man, this stranger (who knows what he could be up to) was not watching his gesturing arms, but reaching out to gently grab them. He was being propelled inward, upward, and then again inward, into the soggiorno of the house with its elegant furniture, oriental rugs on marble floors, relaxing light through Murano glass globes, and that soft sensual scent of Venetian cooking and living. Before he could say anything, he was offered the largest chair in the room, and his host sat down on the sofa opposite him, still rambling on in Italian. All he could muster was his usual word, now modified, "No Italian!"

To this, his host looked amazed, "*No* Italian?" and

added with a laugh "mi, no inglese!"

Then, turning toward the rear of the house, he called "Rosa, grappa, per favore." Almost immediately a smiling woman appeared with a large decanter and three glasses. "Mia consorte," was the added comment, which would have confirmed the man's suspicions if he had understood Italian.

And so, with much smiling, much gesturing, the three of them drank the warming liquor to health, to *salute*, to the future, to *amicizia*. By the time of the last toast, he had become familiar with the faces of their children and grandchildren in the many pictures shown him. He had discovered what a fine baker the wife was with her Torte de Frutta. He admired the skill of the husband's craft as he looked at hand-worked wooden pieces for everything from gondolas to fine furniture. And he had not once said "no."

At long last, which actually seemed more like an extended moment, his hosts rose, and took him to the window to see: "No Acqua!" The passageway was again passable. In a flurry of hugs and two cheek kisses, he descended to the ground floor and out onto the walkway. After a resounding chorus of shared "Ciao", the door closed, and he stood alone in the passage. Looking first right and then left, he suddenly realized that both directions were open for him. In fact, it felt to him like every direction was open to him, like every answer was "yes."

So it is with the ebb and flow of a city whose pulse is more sublime than human, when passages become barriers, and barriers open to reveal passages.

THE STONES

For a city which is built without the usual bedrock-sure footing of earth, it is amazing how much stone has been thrown up upon the mud, silt, reeds, and water of a lagoon to create the image of stability. Or maybe that is why, in an illusion to assuage the deeper knowledge that Venice holds its physical place in the universe on the least substantial basis of any city on earth.

Yet, everywhere you look, stone. The walkways, the canal bulkheads, the buildings, the bridges, the wellheads, the gravestones, and even the waste-receptacles topped with a slab of stone.

But stone is not a warm partner to life. Stone benches spend most of their days warming every so slightly toward comfort. Stone walls keep the winter's chill and the summer's heat as a radiant deposit to add a measure of discomfort to the ambience of any deep winter night or high summer day.

≈≈≈

She had come to Venice in search of stone. Actually stones.

She had come looking to duplicate the marble bathroom she had found in one of the starry hotels of a previous stay. She had come searching for gold jewelry set off by stones of significance more special to her fortunes than to her fates. She had come hoping to find a piece of antiquity represented in stone which she could legally bring back home with her.

So, while others might have spent the time in San Rocco intimately searching the sense of light for some glimpse of their own eternity, she toured hotel bathrooms and dusty stonemason shops. While others might have paused for minutes or hours in San Marco, reviving themselves with the twin spirits of wine and music, she explored tiny alleyways for those special little workshops of jewelers who work to desire, not to custom or even fashion. While others might have watched a sunset across the lagoon from Murano, she dipped into back rooms of dozens of antique stores barely lit by the day's advancing end.

≈≈≈

In the end, she had acquired exactly what she had wanted. In one crate was a marble counter in just the right shade. In another crate was a bust of some nobleman of the 15th century in Venice. In her luggage was a bracelet, necklace, ring, and earrings set that would surely mean another rider on her insurance policy.

As she waited at the rear of her hotel, by the landing and loading area, she watched as first one crate, and then the other, and then her bags were set carefully on the deck of commercial transfer boat, her load being too heavy for any thought of transport by a smaller boat. From the hotel, she would follow the transfer boat down the Grand Canal in a water taxi, the tandem transports heading for the passenger and freight terminal docks at Aeroporto Marco Polo.

She had just boarded the water taxi, and watched the transfer boat get underway ahead, the workers still busily making the cargo fast, when she glimpsed to the sky. It was sunset, and the sky was radiantly red with the highest, thinnest pastel clouds.

In San Marco, at that same moment, a couple who had spent the whole afternoon admiring the picture in San Rocco and then finished off more than a little prosecco at Café Florian to Viennese tempos, were about to step into one of the gondolas for a sunset tour. The two of them, stepping a little too certainly and a little too uncertainly on one of the stones along the canal which had been washed only recently by the flow of the higher-than-usual tide, lost balance, toppling against stone and into water. An ambulance was immediately called when a bloody red was seen against the woman's pastel jacket.

With its two-tone siren screaming, the ambulance rushed down the Grand Canal toward San Marco, all manner of traffic giving way. One boat making the needed sudden turn out of its way was a transfer boat loaded with two crates and some luggage. However, before it could come back to, blocked as it was by other boats pulled aside for the emergency, it was caught fully by the wake of the speeding ambulance. It shuddered a moment, and listed to ride out the wave, when the cargo, not yet fully secured, followed the call of gravity, sliding slowly (some observers would later claim it really did happen in slow motion ... there is a video of it somewhere that proves it) into the depths of the Grand Canal. The two crates sank immediately, with only a high splash as a reminder of their entry; the bags breathed a few gasps and then some more bubbles before following their heavier partners.

And somewhere behind, in a water taxi, a woman laughed, and then said "I wonder where I can find a painting that captures a sunset like this?"

THE HOUSES

If one looks hard enough, one can find urban planning in Venice. Certainly one can find the kind of urban planning that Napoleon brought to the city. And one can look to the newer areas, on the Giudecca and at the tip of Cannaregio for example, where one can find Venetian versions of modern apartment buildings. But along the usual calle or fondamente, one would be hard pressed to find any pattern. The facades vary, the number of stories vary, the height of each story varies, the width varies. Venice is a city of variables when it comes to housing.

A "spacious" apartment on the Grand Canal is about the same size as a "small" apartment in Cannaregio. "Canal" in the description of a house may be modified by "on a", "with views of a", "adjacent to a", "not far from a", and "quietly placed above a", all of which could mean practically anything.

She had rented the apartment near the Rialto, "on the Grand Canal" because she wanted to be able to say she had not denied herself anything.

She had spent most of her life denying herself many things.

She had denied herself most of the pleasures of excess in adolescence because her mother warned her that excesses were the reason the two of them were now alone

The Venice Stories

in the world with few resources. "Waste not, want not," was a household mantra.

She had denied herself the full college experience by living at home. ("A penny saved is a penny earned.")

She had denied herself social connections. ("Don't settle for just anybody.")

She had denied herself career advancement by rejecting job offers that meant moving away. ("Good enough is good enough." and "The grass is never really greener on the other side of the fence.")

When her mother died, she denied herself tears of either sorrow, or relief, or any emotion. ("No use crying over spilled milk.")

When she received her inheritance, which showed that they had never been lacking in resources, that she had never needed to do without, that she could have easily lived on campus, that she was well-off enough to have attracted all the "right" kind of men, that her mother did not need the security of her salary to survive, that her mother could have paid for any amount of care during the illness, she denied herself both tears and shouts of anger.

≈≈≈

When she arrived to take the apartment, it was all she could have wanted. The "house" was actually a Palazzo from the 17th century, now divided into apartments. Her apartment was on the second floor (her American mind still thought of it as the third floor), accessed by a very elegant elevator. The parquet floors shone to mirror the dazzling chandeliers. The fancy plaster work was touched with breaths of blue and gold, while the ceilings were covered with scenes of renaissance delight. Her front sitting room opened onto a balcony with a grand view of the Canal, while her bedroom had its own set of windows, without a balcony, looking upon the same view.

She was surprised those first few days in the apartment at how "at-home" she felt. This was nothing like the house in which she had spent all of her life. This was a house of history, a house of elegance, a house of even a little decadence.

Before she had been housed. She had been "at-home."

But she had never felt like this before.

Everything seemed to be in the right place for her. At night, as she was drifting to sleep, it felt like the house were gently, warmly wrapping itself around her. In the morning, it opened its arms to let in the whole world.

She denied herself none of that world now. If this was to be "her month," then let it truly be hers.

She attended concerts. She explored the art museums. She ate out often, but also cooked for herself with the delightfully fresh foods so nearby in the Rialto markets. She bought herself clothes she liked, stayed out very late some nights listening to jazz, she lingered at tables at every café in San Marco.

It was in the third week of her stay that she met him. He was at the Fiddler's Elbow, nursing a Guinness while she was attacking one head-on. There was live music that night, and she was joining into the singing whole heartedly. He looked over at her and winked, and then joined in too. When a place opened next to him, she slid over. At a break, he said, "I like a woman who does not

The Venice Stories

deny herself anything." She just smiled.

That was only the first evening for the two of them. He, an engineer from England ("a boring sort of family ... only minor title, small estate"), worked in Venice with a consulting firm, of which he was a partner. He loved jazz, fine food, fine art, long walks, Venetian sunsets, and her.

And she did not deny herself the pleasure of his company or the pleasure of her pleasure.

It was on the Monday of the fourth week that she received the call from her company. They were wondering, since she was already in there on vacation, would she be interested at all in a re-assignment to Venice, for at least two years, maybe longer.

On that same afternoon the rental agent came by, to inform her that there was a possibility that she might have to intrude once or twice during the rest of the week as the apartment was about to be put up for sale.

And so that evening, as she stood on her balcony looking over the Grand Canal, she thought to herself about how this house was to become her home, and how this home was to become her house. How by denying herself nothing, she had nothing she needed to deny. And just then she heard, echoing over the water, the sound of a woman's laugh.

She knew just how that woman felt, she thought, laughing at life.

And she did not deny herself a long, long joyous laugh.

THE BOATS

Randolph W.B. Becker

Venice cannot exist as a city without her boats.

It was by boat that the earliest settlers came to the area to avoid the terror of the barbarians on the mainland.

It was by boat that the essential goods arrived needed to build a city in the sea.

It was by boat that the great trading empire that was Venice ventured forth.

It was by boat, the mighty ships of war built in her own Arsenal, that the empire was protected.

It was by boat that the spoils of conquest, in bronze and gold and bone and mosaic, arrived to grace the islands.

And it is only by boat that the modern city can exist.

Boats to ferry travelers. Boats to deliver goods. Boats to collect the garbage. Boats to repair the canals. Boats to transfer the mail.

And seemingly at the bottom rung of the hierarchy of boats is the Traghetto. This step-cousin of the more elegant gondola is a workhorse, but a workhorse of convenience not necessity. Ferrying people from one side of the Grand Canal to the other, these large, unadorned, oft-worn-out-looking crafts invite people to stand for a short passage across the canal powered by two oarsmen. Of course, these people could have found their way to the other side by crossing one of the bridges or using the *Vaporetti*.

≈≈≈

It was into just such a boat that the man and woman stepped about midday. He was not so certain about this, but she was pretty adamant. It was simple, would help them avoid a long walk, was cheaper than a waterbus, and would save time. So, unsteady on his feet as ever, he approached the steps to the boat. One of the oarsmen shouted for him to stop. "Signore, not to step on those wet stones," pointing to one of the steps slightly greenish in tint. He was more than glad to oblige the suggestion, and trod instead on the wooden steps. As he placed one foot over into the boat, he felt that moment of panic that he always felt around water. Maybe it was a result of some childhood experience at the lake where his father, a daring boater, would show his son the limits of the small outboard motorboat. He didn't know. But he did know that with one foot on land and one foot on sea, he liked the land footing better.

≈ ≈ ≈

"Go ahead, dear!" his wife said into his ear, and he did as he was told. This was their first day in Venice, and he was not about to ruin it this early in the day. He proceeded to walk forward in the boat, and then turned around to face the shore, as he had seen the locals doing. Then his wife came and did the same in front of him. The boat was becoming crowded, and they pushed in a little closer. Her hair was in his face, and he was surprised that he was not annoyed by this. In fact, there in the sun upon the water, he found the scent of her hair almost intoxicating. He put his hands on either side of her at her waist, and gently kissed one ear. She looked back at him with a smile, and then put her hands on his in a wonderfully loving way.

Maybe this trip was going to be different.

Usually when they went anywhere together, it was

with the best of intention and the worst of execution. If something could go wrong, not only would it go wrong but it would go wrong to them.

It was so bad that he had taken to dreading doing anything new. Doing the tried and true had enough pitfalls, so why chance something new?

And it always felt, in the midst of those trials and tribulations, that adversity did not bring them together, but sent them apart.

Yet, here they were, in a city they had never been in before, with the sun and the water and her hair and her hands, heralding that this time would be different.

He braced himself for the departure from the dock and was surprised that all he could feel was a gentle gliding action, then a turning-about, and then the smoothest of sensations as they crossed the busy canal. At the far side, carefully disembarking to avoid the slippery stones, he looked at his wife and beamed. Taking her hand in his, with a quick kiss to her forehead, he led them on their way. They were off to see what there was to see at San Rocco. But first, how about a light lunch at an outdoor café? She quickly agreed.

The afternoon was as delicious as its approach had been. Together they marveled at the Venetian masters' uses of light and shadow, of form and field. As the first of the evening bells began to ring, he suggested they return across the canal the same way they had come. His wife seemed surprised but willing. "Why, it sounds like you have changed your mind," was what she said, to which he quickly replied, "about the boat, yes, but not about you,"

The Venice Stories

which was followed equally quickly with a rather startlingly passionate kiss.

"O, my!" was all she could muster.

So, again to the steps by the canal, again into the boat, but this time he had no hesitation in stepping in. He was grinning! This is wonderful!

This time he let his wife enter first, and now it was her turn to stand behind him on an equally crowded traghetto. Her lips touched the back of his neck, but her hands, well they were not on his waist.

They were almost giddy getting out of the boat. Hand in hand, they strolled without much purpose until, at last, they found themselves in San Marco. The orchestras were playing, the place was a alive with sounds and sights and people. He gallantly proposed some wine at one of the cafés. She accepted with pleasure. He asked for a suggestion of something thoroughly Venetian. "Prosecco."

So, they enjoyed the early evening together in San Marco, whistling along with the tunes, gazing at each other, just plain smiling a lot, and ordering a second bottle of the wine.

As the shadows were beginning to lengthen, the waiter came to their table to inform them they might want to think about dinner plans. It seems there was a prediction of *acqua alta*, the high water. "Soon those drain in San Marco will begin to fill with water, and this Piazza becomes very wet."

"What do most people here do then?" he asked.

And he was told that some go home, and some go to their favorite restaurant, to eat way the several hours while the water is at its highest.

"But, who wants to be inside on a night like this?" she asked, pointing to the sky just now becoming tinged with a red fire.

Her husband surprised her by asking, "Can you still take a gondola ride at such a time?"

And he was assured that, yes, it was very possible ... and probably less crowded.

So, he looked at her and said, "Dear, this has been one of my happiest days of my life, and this has been one of the most wonderful days we have ever spent together. Let's do it up right. Come boating with me."

And with a vigorous shake of her head, for words would have been too hard to speak through all of her emotions, she agreed with him.

The bill was paid, the waiter well tipped, and then they stood to go. O dear, that wine had its magic.

"Signore, be careful!" the waiter warned.

"We will, we will," the two answered in unison.

And then the two of them, with a slight wobble in their steps, made their way out of San Marco toward the water. And he knew, he just knew, that today was going to be one of those days, finally, when everything worked for them. After all, hadn't he mastered the boats?

THE CHURCH

Some come to Venice to see the art.
Some come to Venice to see the churches.
Some come to Venice to see the art and the churches.
She came to Venice to see the art and avoid the churches.
That's not easy to do.
But her life had not ever been easy.
It always seemed hard.
She probably liked it that way. In fact, she probably made it that way.
But, she always blamed her hard life on God, a God she did not believe in.
She had not believed in God as long as she could remember.
She could remember when she was a little girl, was she three or four, sitting on the long wooden seat. She was looking up at the men, always men, at the front, with unusual clothes on. Big, big decorations, too big, too scary for a small person. The people around her sitting, standing, sitting, standing, talking, singing (but when she would try to talk or sing or stand, she was told to sit and be quiet). But most of all, she remembered how hard it all was: the seat, the sitting still, the being quiet, the not

letting on how scary a place it was.

When she was about six, one of her schoolmates told her all about God and heaven and hell and Jesus and the saints ... and all she could think of was that it was just too hard to remember all of that. On late Friday afternoons she would watch people rushing to be home before sundown, like something awful and terrible was chasing them. If I were being chased by something that big and bad, I would want to run home too, she thought. It would be hard to be running like that all the time.

When she was seven, her father went away for a long time. Her mother told her that he was sick and needed to get well. Her grandmother told her she should pray a lot. When she asked Nana why she should pray, she was told so God could make him better. So each night she would fall to her knees beside her bed, and try to remember the words she heard sitting on that long hard seat. They all sounded so foreign. She said the ones she could remember, and made up some more.

But when her father came home looking like a shadow not a man, she smiled for him but inside she cried. Either her prayers did not work, or God did not work. She knew she loved her Daddy more than anything in the world, so her prayers must have been very good. So, if it were not her prayers ...

Later that year, just before December with all of its holiday busyness, her father began coughing one day, and could not stop. Behind a half closed door, she stood and watched while the ambulance men took her father away. That was the last time she saw him. When he was sleeping in the long wooden box, and she was sitting very quietly, very long, on the long hard seat, she could not see him, not with her eyes anyway.

All around her people were speaking words she did not understand.

All around her people were crying, which she did understand.

Then, when she could finally get off that hard seat, the people were touching her, talking to her.

People were saying that she had to trust God, that God would take care of her father, which she did not understand.

People were crying as they said it, and that she did understand – they were lying.

No, they were not lying, there were just repeating a lie, which was even worse. They just said what other people had told them to say to a little girl of seven whose father had died. They spread the lie about God taking care of her father.

But she knew.

She knew her prayers were not listened to.

She knew that God made people uncomfortable.

She knew that God made people run scared.

She knew that God made rules that no one could follow without making a mistake.

She knew that mistakes get punished.

She knew that God had taken her father.

And so, she knew, that there was a God she did not believe in.

She knew it with a fierce faith.

No God!

≈≈≈

How that God-who-wasn't would play out in her life became a game with her, a kind of faith gymnastics.

And to be in shape for the competition, which could come most unexpectedly, she had to practice.

If all those who believed in God had to study, pray, and worship, just to get the kind of God she did not believe in, her God-who-wasn't needed even more attention. There were no familiar routines to follow. No holy books full of prayers known for their piety. No organized pilgrimages to sacred ground. No rites of passage into adulthood. She did, of course, have her own holy books, and her own sacred ground, and her own rituals and rites. They were known only to her, observed only by her, understood only by her. Her religious practice became the practice of the pioneer, the one who believes they are breaking the virgin soil, forgetting the æons of seedlings who have come before.

The role of pioneer became more dominant than the specific elements in her preteen years. When her classmates all thought about baseball, she spoke about soccer. When the girls in her classes would be talking about dresses for the eighth grade dance, she would talk about boots for a weekend hike. They spoke of Nancy Drew, she of Amelia Earhart. They of Bar or Bat Mitzvahs and confirmations, she of vision quests.

By the time she was thirteen, she had become her own best, and probably only, friend. Her mother was never the same after her father had died. Her mother had dated several men, but none seemed to match a recalled memory of perfection. Silently the daughter rejoiced each time her mother released one of the men back into the great pool of eligibility. She was not ready for a new person, especially a step-father, in her life.

Since her mother had become like a new person in those years, not at all like the woman who had been wife to her father, she had little room in her life for her mother either. The usual teenage battling between mothers and daughters was absent, replaced by a very empty silence. They were like two lunar orbits intertwining in space but around two distinctly different planets, passing in space and time, but seemingly having no relationship to each other, the gravity of their own lives overcoming any attraction (or repulsion) their passing might have occasioned.

≈≈≈

She was alone on a vast plane of existence, a pioneer out under the broad skies. And under that plane, and above those skies, she knew there was nothing. Earth and sky were enough for her.

In high school she found that sometimes others live on the prairie as well. A distant smoke signal would arise. Maybe it was in an English class, when another student would introduce an author whose obscurity she thought she had read well enough to assure privacy. Or in science, when another would push the limits of some theoretical point beyond where the teacher was willing or able to go, and she would hear her own thoughts echoing in the words of another. Or in history, when someone else would ask if

The Venice Stories

it were not possible to think of the period of the from 500 to 1500 as something other than about the church, and she would find herself saying a quiet "bravo".

Those slight glimmers of sociability on the horizon of her extended plane of being gave her both hope and sadness. Hope that she was not alone, that others might also be able to see what she saw; sadness, that maybe she was not as unique as she hoped she was.

It was in the late winter of her junior year of high school that another student, a boy she had not noticed before, commented while passing her in the hallway "Thus spake Zarathustra!" in a loud pronouncement. How did he know that in her book bag was *The Essential Nietzsche*?

In the weeks to come, he would bewilder her. Not every day, but often enough, he would pass her in the halls and say something indicating that either he was reading her mind or pilfering her locker.

She decided on a ploy, and checked out from the city library some books unlike her usual reading matter. These she divided between her book bag and her locker. Then, she waited.

A day or two passed, and no comment. Finally, he did speak, but this time only to say something that related to theme of a *New York Times* op-ed piece she had been reading at home the night before. Nothing about those decoys. Nothing!

Who was this guy? What did he know? How did he know?

She decided bold action was necessary, and so the next time she saw him, she said simply "Hi, how's it going?" He looked surprised, and a little crestfallen, and only murmured "Oh, OK, I guess" before hurrying on.

When she tried another attempt to reach out to him, a smile and a quick "hi", he looked equally bewildered.

Now "Who was this guy?" was replaced with "What's with this guy?"

The spring break came, and so she did not see him at all for 10 days. When school started up, the talk of the junior class was the upcoming "Ring Dance" at which the class members who had ordered their school rings would receive them. This was the highlight of the junior class spring social season. Posters were everywhere.

Walking the social gauntlet the hallways had become, she saw him coming, and, without thinking, blurted out "You know, a ring dance is just mindless tribal imitation."

And he stopped, looked her in the eye, and replied "And school rings are mere pretentious totems of transitory connections."

Maybe those smoke signals were not as far away as the horizon.

≈≈≈

In the weeks to come, she and he would venture a comment as they passed, never anything cordial, polite, safe, meaningless. No, they spoke what was going on in their minds. Stream of consciousness hallway encounters of the teenage kind.

Finally, surprising even herself, she said one day as her offering "Could we sometime say something other than one sentence each?"

He smiled, and responded, "Would you like more ... or

less?" and then winked.

That did it.

Two can be pioneers on the prairie of life together.

And like many a pioneer household, they became inseparable. To face the great challenges and dangers of living on the edge of existence, away from the comfort and convenience of society, but also away from the confines and constraints of that society, they needed each other desperately.

His life had not been shaped by doubt and loss.

He had never worried about a God-who-wasn't, growing up in a non-religious family. He had never sat on a long, hard bench. He had never worried about heavens and hells. In his family, thought was more important than belief, action more important than faith, love more important than obedience.

But he had also never had to deal with the intimacy of loss through death. Amazingly not only were both his parents alive, but he had four grandparents and all eight great-grandparents. As the endpoint of a long family history of only children, he had no extended family beyond that except one great-great aunt living at a distance and some cousins of numerical quality and positions removed as to be meaningless, and since they were on his mother's mother's mother's side, without even a name to share.

If her cup was filled from losing, his was filled from keeping. And they surprised each other at how similar the two cupfuls looked.

Out on their prairie, out at their pioneer outpost, they often sat for hours and talked. It was like they knew what would be said before the other said it. As much as both of them laughed at some of the pop psychology material that was coming out, they referred to each other as soul mates (although at times they would joke that they would probably end up as cellmates, of the padded variety).

Senior year was the usual whirl of stress and exhilaration for them, from SAT's to application essays ("dare we tell the truth?") to AP courses to that moment in April when the fat and the skinny envelopes appeared.

They had a pact. Each of them would have the mail gathered in their homes each day and placed in a sealed envelope. After school they would get their envelopes and meet, and together they would discover what had been sent.

The first few days offered nothing one day, and only meaningless armed forces recruiting attempts another, and a letter about graduation requirements from the high school another. Then came the day when the sealed envelopes were fat, heavy, promising, although they both teased the other about mail order catalogues.

When the seals had been broken, and the contents spread before them, eight envelopes yielded each of them the choice of three universities that wanted them, two of which would provide enough financial aid to make it possible, and one which said, "Sorry".

And one of those that said yes and offered aid was the same for both of them.

So, they were faced with the wonderful and painful choice – to continue to be pioneers together, or to go their separate ways. They chose to explore the future together.

The Venice Stories

That first year in college was challenging for them, more socially than intellectually. They soon found that there were other people who liked to share the same great prairie they had staked as their own. Others too loved the obscure books they loved, others too had a disdain for social convention, others too lived without a reference to God, others too would rather work the unbroken soil then simply trod the ruts of time.

They found they loved each other even more for the way that each was able to let others into their circle, their compound, without feeling threatened or needy. If in finding each other they had found how not to be alone, in finding these others they had found community. Their sense of connection was expanding. And with it a recognition that in true connection, you always gain, but never have to lose.

What you truly have, you can never lose.

What you do not have, you cannot lose.

≈≈≈

In their junior year, he began to have headaches. They joked it was probably from all the studying. Both were Art History majors, spending endless hours both reading analysis and pouring over prints and slides of art. He had his eyes checked and his prescription changed. It did not help. He saw a chiropractor who tried some adjustments. He changed his diet to more whole foods. His headaches continued. Finally, the university health clinic sent him to a neurologist for a work up. And the neurologist sent him to an oncologist.

Nineteen days shy of his twentieth birthday, he died of

a brain tumor. As he lay there, in his final hours of consciousness, she looked him in the eye and said "Dammit, now, again, I can only have real conversations with myself."

His head moved slowly from right to left and back again, and responded "Not if you listen really hard," followed by a half-successful wink.

Fortunately, his family was who they were. There was no service for him. No body lying in a wooden box. No prayers in strange languages. No people telling anyone it will be OK through their own tears. Nothing hard to get through like all of that would have been.

It was just life that was hard.

And if there were a God, which there isn't, she thought, it is all his fault.

≈≈≈

Her prediction became almost thoroughly true. The community to which they had connected as a couple now seemed either empty to her alone or unsure how to be there for only her. She could not tell which it was, but that did not matter. Now, she was, once again, the only person with whom she could have a real conversation.

"Senior year," she said to herself, "will be either hell or something else. Kiddo, it's your choice!"

So she made it something else. She over-enrolled, and still got a 4.0. She was elected to Phi Beta Kappa, received her diploma *summa cum laude*, and was offered a graduate fellowship to continue her art history studies abroad. The only thing she regretted about that year was the graduation ceremony, where she knew that the only

The Venice Stories

two important people in her life other than herself would not be there. When she heard that the graduation speaker was to be a highly placed religious official, she decided that the God-who-wasn't was telling her she needed to be somewhere else.

So as her classmates were processing down the aisle of a college yard, she as walking down a jetway onto her flight to the future. She had decided to tour Europe in the months before her graduate studies would begin. To finally see all those works whose reproductions were etched into her mind. To see those expressions of the human spirit which he and she had shared so often. To see all that energy and beauty which had been, in her opinion, wasted on Madonnas and Saints and Saviors and Prophets and Heavens and Hells, when the edge of the horizon of the eternal prairie called out for their expression even more boldly.

"What if they had painted the future, and not the past?" she wondered to herself.

She had already been to London, Amsterdam, Paris, Madrid, Seville, Barcelona, Roma, Milano, and Firenze, before coming to Venezia. Friends had told her to do it that way, for the shock of the other cities would be too great after the effect of Venezia on her spirit. She laughed when they said this, thinking of how much in her life she had learned to deal with on her own, with her own spirit.

Yet she suddenly knew what they meant when she walked from her train, out of Ferrovia S. Lucia, to gaze upon the Grand Canal before her. This was not a city of museums, but a city as a museum. Even the everyday houses were pieces of the grand overall puzzle of art. And so many elements, of earth, air, water, and fire, blending in ways she could not have imagined until she stepped down from the station, and onto a waterbus.

She regretted that she was running behind her schedule. She had lingered here and there longer than anticipated, sometimes provoked by changing gallery hours, sometimes by the habitual strikes on all manner of transportation, and less frequently than she would have liked by her own inner demand to stay with a piece of art longer than she had planned.

So her days passed in all of the great places of art. The galleries. The Palazzos. But when it came to churches, she had learned early on that she had to be careful. True, much of Europe's art is in churches, and churches are places that like to have services now and then. Services whose focus was always that God-who-wasn't.

If she chose to see the art in a church during its services, she would be expected to sit quietly on a long, hard bench while someone spoke in a language foreign to her, all trying to tell her in words she could not understand, about how God would take care of them. That she could not face. Life was hard enough, without throwing that in.

Yet, by her last day in Venezia, (and it truly had to be her last day in Venezia, for if she delayed any more the fellowship would be forfeited) she realized she had one last painting she had to see. In fact, she saved this one for last, because it is one that she and he most discussed when finding its reproduction in some work. It was the Bellini,

Virgin Mary with Christ Child, the one in which the child hovers magically above the palm of his mother, suspended in time and space, different from other human beings. They had joked about telekinesis, and hidden wires, and how there was one person who would never find a bench hard. Still, through all of their jokes, something brought them back to that painting.

So, to the "Tintoretto" church of Madonna dell'Otro she went in search not of Tintoretto, but of Bellini. This was to be her benediction to Venice, to the trip, to everything past, and her valediction to her life unfolding, an act of her own making and her own choosing.

As she landed at the motoscafo stop *Orto*, she heard the ringing of bells in the distance, and thought nothing of it. Bells in Venice are like car horns in New York.

As she made her way from the Lagoon, she realized that she was gradually joining in an ever-growing procession of people of all ages moving in her direction. Turning into the campo where the church sits, she realized these people were not on their way to market, as she supposed, but to church. All of her careful planning was for nothing. A service was about to begin. Maybe she could quickly go in, see it, and leave. So, she entered through the doors into what would, in a few minutes, become sacred space. After her eyes adjusted for the light difference, she looked about for where the painting should be, and realized that more than half of the people coming in to worship were headed to that immediate area. Was it the painting? She moved with them and then stepped back, for where the guide book said the painting should be was only a very bare wall.

She consulted her guidebook again. No, this was right. But what? A gentle hand touched her elbow. She looked at first over, and then finally realizing, down, to where a very old looking woman was standing beside her, the woman's eyes damp with tears. "Bellini," she said, "Perduto!"

"What, lost?" What does woman mean? She did not realize that she spoke the first part of her thought out loud.

To her left a much younger man, probably about her age said quietly, "It is gone, the Bellini, stolen, lost ..."

And upon hearing that she found herself dropping onto the long, hard bench. And for once, she had nothing to say, not even to herself.

Into that silence came music, the beginning of the Mass. When they stood, she stood, and when they spoke, she listened to the mysterious words and tried to echo them. She did not know why, she just did.

And then as the Priest intoned more of the Mass, she looked around her. She saw people of all ages, all stations of life, alone and together, all in this place. Some were looking at the priest, some were looking at their own hands, some had their eyes closed, but more were looking at one of the many paintings, and still more were looking at a bare wall where a painting had been. And in many an eye she caught a twinkle of moisture, a look she had not seen in so many people since her father's funeral. But none of them was telling her it would be OK. None of them was speaking. In the silence of the time for prayer, no one, not congregant nor priest was speaking. And then she heard it, heard it as real as day: "So maybe he just flew up all the

The Venice Stories

way, and they had to take down the picture because it would look stupid without him in it," just as he would have said it. And suddenly the bench was no longer hard for her, for she felt like she was floating above it, as if above the palm of someone who loved her. In her mind's eye she saw a puff of smoke off on the end of the plane of her sight. And then another. And then another. With that her eyes filled with tears that told her it would be OK, that she would be OK, truly OK. Tears still streaming down her face, she emerged into the daylight, into the future, from the church of a God-who-wasn't and also a God-who-was-waiting-to-be.

↗ ↗ ↗

Randolph W.B. Becker

Bonus

By going to the New Atlantian Library website (NewAtlantianLibrary.com) and entering this password in to the Bonus Reward Section, you can read a totally new short story by Randolph W.B. Becker – for **free!**

AA1034

About the Author

Randolph W.B. Becker is an inveterate traveler who always seeks to be more a temporary resident than a tourist. You will most often find him on public transit, eating at neighborhood restaurants, finding what you do when you get lost, and braving barely-known languages to converse with newly-found friends over a glass of red wine. When not on the move, he lives in Key West, Conch Republic.

RevRandy@spiritualpersistence.com

The New Atlantian Library

NewAtlantianLibrary.com or
AbsolutelyAmazingEbooks.com
or AA-eBooks.com

Printed in Great Britain
by Amazon